Action Research
PRIMER

PETER LANG
New York • Washington, D.C./Baltimore • Bern
Frankfurt am Main • Berlin • Brussels • Vienna • Oxford

Patricia H. Hinchey

Action Research
PRIMER

PETER LANG
New York • Washington, D.C./Baltimore • Bern
Frankfurt am Main • Berlin • Brussels • Vienna • Oxford

Library of Congress Cataloging-in-Publication Data

Hinchey, Patricia H.
Action research primer / Patricia H. Hinchey.
p. cm. — (Peter Lang primers)
Includes bibliographical references.
1. Action research in education. I. Title.
LB1028.24.H56   370.7'2—dc22   2007044387
ISBN 978-0-8204-9527-9

Bibliographic information published by **Die Deutsche Bibliothek**.
Die Deutsche Bibliothek lists this publication in the "Deutsche
Nationalbibliografie"; detailed bibliographic data is available
on the Internet at http://dnb.ddb.de/.

Cover design by Clear Point Designs

© 2008 Peter Lang Publishing, Inc., New York
29 Broadway, 18th floor, New York, NY 10006
www.peterlang.com

Printed in the United States of America

Contents

Some Basics and Some History

Introduction to the Concept of Action Research

Some Basics

To understand what action research (AR) is, it's helpful first to sweep some common but misleading mental images of *research* out of the way. One teacher has described the stereotypical picture as "Big R" research, characterized by "long hours in the library, notes that could fill a novel, and a bibliography several pages long.... [with] tension and stress lurking in the shadows" (Hubbard and Power, 1999, xiv). A common alternative picture features a scientist surrounded by tubes, or maybe cages, slaving away in a laboratory night and day to verifiably pin down the *truth* of something. Neither image is likely to hold much appeal for the typical educator—but then, neither image bears any resemblance to the action research process. Action research (AR) involves no helpless dependence on or abject reverence for authorities, no white lab coats, no laboratory, no bells and salivating dogs, no single-minded pursuit of truth.

The image of research as stressful suffering is likely the product of an unhappy experience with a "research paper" in school—a very different task for a very different purpose than action research. The images of *research* as a

scientific, laboratory-oriented activity producing verifiable results comes from decades of educational research that intended to identify the "one best way" to teach. Historically, experts outside the classroom, usually university professors, have conducted such research through laboratory experiments. Their intent was to uncover the best teaching strategies and then offer prescriptions to classroom teachers—a research process that Cochran-Smith and Lytle (1993) refer to as "outside-in," because it features researchers outside of classrooms designing practice for teachers inside them.

Of course, the work of these outside researchers has provided much useful information on a wide variety of topics—that class size affects learning, for example, or that teachers need to give students more than a few seconds to think about questions. However, many studies in this tradition have also caused practitioners to protest "But children *aren't* dogs," or "But laboratories *aren't* classrooms." Generations of teachers have objected that one-size-fits-all research prescriptions for teaching did not and could not fit every individual student any more than size six clothing could fit every child aged six, or that one type of clothing could be suitable for every child. Some teaching guidelines developed in traditional research are, as teachers know, equivalent to deciding that all children, including those in Florida, are best dressed in snowsuits.

In calling attention to the variations of real world children and classrooms, critics of traditional research methodology have pointed out that despite its usefulness in some areas, it also has distinct limits. However useful its generalizations may sometimes be, traditional educational research cannot tell any individual teacher what exactly will work best in a particular classroom at a particular moment with a specific class or student. Each classroom is a world unto itself with widely varied students, cultures, values, languages, goals, personalities, constraints and opportunities. Any and all of these factors—along with emotional states, interpersonal dynamics, and even the weather—make any teaching moment a unique one that calls for a teacher's expertise in choosing among possible strategies. This is a key area where action research is crucially different from traditional research efforts: the researchers are not outsiders, like university professors. Instead, they are insiders, citizens of a school or other community, who explore improvements in areas they think important. And, the goals of the research are determined by the people who conduct it; action research is a process that pursues improvement in "practical situations…without substantively prescribing objectives to be achieved" (Herbert et al., 2002, p. 127). Goals, as well as researchers, come from the inside rather than outside.

When teachers engage in action research, the questions they ask and the improvements they pursue are as varied as teachers and classrooms themselves. For example, teachers I worked with recently posed the following questions about their own classrooms and practice:

- Children should not be crying in schools. How can I reduce my students' stress about mandated state tests?
- I know I don't teach geography well, partly because I don't know and/or like it. Would learning improve if I turned responsibility for teaching it over to students?
- I worry whether students are learning the most important lessons I can offer them. How well does the curriculum I choose align with my students' interests and needs?
- I have a student with a disability who seems unengaged and whose aide and family appear to be doing her work for her. What can I do to improve her learning?
- What stereotypes do my students hold about science, about who is good in science and who is bad in science, especially in terms of gender?
- Why are students who enroll in the college classes I teach consistently, predominantly male?

As that last question indicates, the usefulness of action research is not limited to particular levels of teaching. Teachers from pre-kindergarten through graduate school have employed action research to better understand their classrooms and options. The questions above, for example, merely hint at the many areas open to inquiry: students' emotional health, quality of academic content, pedagogical strategies, alignment of curriculum with students' interests, the needs of an individual student, cultural influence on student beliefs, and gender issues. As we'll soon see, the questions can also be much larger, asking about ways to improve conditions outside of classrooms as well as within them.

Action research

a process of systematic inquiry, usually cyclical, conducted by those inside a community rather than by outside experts; its goal is to identify action that will generate some improvement the researcher believes important.

Once the stereotypes of *research* are swept away, the essential characteristics of **action research** are fairly simply stated:

- It is conducted by those inside a community (teachers, administrators, community members) rather than by outside experts.
- It pursues improvement or better understanding in some area the researcher considers important.
- It involves systematic inquiry, which includes information gathering, analysis and reflection.
- It leads to an action plan, which frequently generates a new cycle of the process.

The work of the teacher cited above who wanted to improve geography teaching and learning in her classroom provides an easily explained example.

First, the teacher—whom I'll call Sue—thought carefully about her classroom experience and identified an area that she wanted to improve. After considering her past efforts, the state of her own knowledge, and her colleagues' comments on constructivist teaching methods and democratic classrooms, Sue wondered whether learning might improve if she turned geography teaching over to students. She created an assignment that did so. Then, she carefully collected information on what happened as students planned, presented and discussed their lessons; analyzed the data she had collected, identifying strengths and weakness of what occurred; and, made changes to the assignment based on her analysis. Next year, she will try out the revised assignment and repeat the research process to determine if she is satisfied with the results. It's not enough to plan and implement an action: its results must be systematically analyzed to determine whether desired improvements have occurred and whether unintended consequences, good or bad, turned up as well. For this reason, the process is generally described as being **cyclical**. This teacher's process might be described as seen in Figure 1.

Cyclical

an ongoing process in which the same steps are continually repeated.

Several models to describe the essential nature of this research cycle have been suggested. One is a helix comprised of three essential and recurring acts: look, think, act (Stringer, 2004). Another three-phase process embeds similar ideas in different terms: reflect, act, evaluate (Hendricks, 2006). Still another proposes a cycle of initiation, detection and judgment (Schmuck, 2006). Whatever the specifics of the model, however, theorists conceive AR as a process in

FIGURE 1: SAMPLE ACTION RESEARCH CYCLE FOR A CLASSROOM STUDY

Identify concern (weak geography teaching) → Collect and analyze data to clarify situation (consider personal attributes, thoughts of colleagues) → Plan and implement action (assign geography teaching to students) → Collect and analyze data on effects (notes as groups worked, pre-and post-surveys of student thinking, evaluations of teaching products and discussions) → Identify remaining concerns (students used poor information sources and wanted more choice of topic) → Plan and implement action (revise assignment to correct weaknesses and build on strengths and assign next year) → Collect and analyze data on effects (repeat of earlier effort) → and so on . . .

---

which one step leads to another over and over in a continual improvement process. The end segment of any cycle frequently generates the first segment of the next one.

Of course, teachers do this kind of analytical thinking about their practice informally every day (Was John confused? Was there really enough time for that activity? Should this lesson have come earlier or later?). AR is a way to build upon what practitioners do naturally by formalizing this informal habit. The advantage to formalizing the process is that in providing more structure, the action research process focuses the participant's attention on one area for an extended time and ensures not only that new actions result but that they are evaluated on the basis of systematically collected data from real world experience.

Some Variations

While much of the above discussion of action research includes widely accepted generalities, it is important to be aware that there are significant variations in how researchers, theorists and practitioners think about and define the action research process. A growing number of alternative terms reflect such variation: "In the literature and in popular usage, terms such as 'research,' 'action,' 'collaborative,' **'critical,'** and 'inquiry' have been combined with one another and with the term "teacher" to signal a wide range of meanings and purposes" (Cochran-Smith and Lytle, 1993, p. xiii). One educational action research text that focuses primarily on teacher research, for example, differentiates among six different types of research teachers may conduct: teacher research, classroom research, action research, teacher action research, classroom action research, and collaborative

Critical (emancipatory or liberatory)

term/s indicating a concern with unequal power arrangements and a conception of education as activism in the interest of social justice; such work is often significantly grounded in the work of Brazilian educator and theorist Paulo Freire.

action research (Holly et al., 2005, p. 49). Another lists four different types: collaborative action research, critical action research, classroom action research, and participatory action research (Hendricks, 2006). Each list leaves out still other possibilities: teacher inquiry, classroom inquiry, practitioner research and so on.

The proliferation of terms makes obvious that action research has come to mean different things for different people, and the differences are significant. As Cochran-Smith and Lytle (1993) note, they signify important differ-ences in key areas including: which research **paradigm** is appropriate for action research; who rightfully produces knowledge and who uses it; and who or what should ben-efit from the research work. Obviously, such differences in conceptual thinking lead to very different definitions and forms of practice. In order to develop "clarity of purpose among those who would use the term" (Noffke, 1997, p. 308), it is important for those interested in AR to examine the variations and think through what exactly they will do—and why—if they choose to do *action research*. As a preliminary to the fuller discussion, however, a sampling of diverse terminology can offer some insight into variations.

At a simplistic surface level, any term that names an element of education—*teacher* research or *classroom* research, for example—indicates that the work is being done in education, distinguishing it from efforts in other areas where action research is also popular, like business and social work. The term t*eacher research* also indicates that it is teachers (not administrators or consultants) who are the researchers. The term *teacher inquiry,* in avoiding the word *research,* suggests that the work is intended to benefit the practitioner without any particular concern for contributing to a knowledge base. Others would argue that the term *practitioner inquiry* is a better descriptor for the work of an individual teacher focused on his or her own classroom, and that the term *action research* should be reserved for collaborative efforts involving more than one person (Stringer, 2004). Others use the term *collabora-tive action research* to indicate the expectation for group work. Moreover, if the word *critical* is added to any of these terms—as in *critical action research* or *critical teacher research*—it signals that the work will focus on social issues, especially unequal power arrangements and social justice.

Paradigm

a world view; a set of theoretical or philosophical beliefs.

Obviously, there is no universally accepted definition for action research or educational action research because there are so many variations on the concept. Therefore, "action research is best thought of as a large family, one in which beliefs and relationships vary greatly...[as] a group of ideas emergent in various contexts" (Noffke, 1997, p. 306). And yet, with all of that said, the essential characteristics identified above do apply broadly: Action research is a process of systematic inquiry, usually cyclical, conducted by those inside a community rather than outside experts; its goal is to identify action that will generate improvement the researchers believe important. That can serve as a working definition, then, with the caveat that this core idea can become many different things when translated to practice. As will be evident later, common variations in conception and practice include: whether one or more than one researcher is involved; whether, in addition to practitioners, others—like community members or consultants—are involved; how data is collected, analyzed, reported and used; and whether the purpose of the research is to contribute to or to change the field of educational research itself, or to change the teacher, the teaching, the students, the classroom, the school—or the world beyond the classroom door.

In the Beginning: Some Key Figures

As is true in any field, the seeds of contemporary thinking, including some of its major variations, can be traced to key influential figures. Because important early work was done by a variety of people whose work had different emphases and purposes, many of today's action research "family members" have features inherited from various ancestors. Following is a brief portrait gallery of some key figures whose work shaped today's conceptions and who are frequently referred to in much of the action research literature. Familiarity with some ideas from these early theorists and researchers provides some foundation for understanding action research's contemporary popularity and trends.

John Dewey

During the early twentieth century, John Dewey was such a prolific writer and influential figure that many later developments in education have connections to his work. Although his name does not appear consistently in action

research literature, some writers do note that important features of what we know as action research are outlined in his work (Holly et al., 2005; Tomal, 2003; Schmuck, 2006, for example). Like many others of his time, Dewey believed that scientific inquiry and theory have a definite place in education. Unlike them, however, he argued that research shouldn't be done solely by outsiders on behalf of teachers, but also by the insiders, teachers themselves.

While others imagined teachers as uncritical recipients of what expert researchers deemed best practices, Dewey argued that research findings need to be tested and adjusted by teachers in the field. Situations differ, and what works best in one case may not work best in another. He compared the process to that used by a doctor, who is familiar with existing research findings but nevertheless treats each patient as an individual for whom common diagnoses and prescriptions may or may not apply: "after all, cases are like, not identical.... Indications of the standardized or general methods used in like cases by others—particularly by those who are already experts—are of worth or of harm according as they make [a practitioner's] personal reaction more intelligent or as they induce a person to dispense with exercise of his own judgment" (1916, Chapter 13, "Method as General and Individual," ¶4).

Dewey challenged the idea that teachers are a kind of puppet whose strings are pulled by outside researchers. Instead, he characterized teachers as active agents who need to be familiar with the research findings of others, but who are capable of—indeed, responsible for—deciding for themselves what findings might or might not apply to specific situations in their own practice. In fact, Dewey expected teachers to do a great deal of such thinking on their own as a necessary and integral part of teaching, which he considered to a "reflective" activity—an idea later significantly built upon by Donald Schön in his influential work *The Reflective Practitioner* (1983), which also is frequently referenced in action research literature.

Moreover, Dewey's description of scientific method as it applies to the classroom still constitutes a good characterization of the action research process. The model he advanced begins in a practitioner's "perplexity, confusion, doubt" and moves through analysis and hypothesis to an action plan for improvement that must be "tried in the world" (1916, Chapter 11, "Reflection in Experience," ¶7).

Today, Dewey's "confusion, perplexity, doubt" appear in AR guides as the source of teachers' action research questions—or "wonderings" (Dana & Yendol-Silva, 2003). More important for the concept of action research, however, is Dewey's insistence that any idea for action must be tested in the world of practice. Dewey was among the first to insist that educational research must occur not only in the lab but in the world. Teachers, he argued, have a significant role to play in developing, testing, and adapting findings that they try out in their classrooms. While he valued traditional research findings, he believed them to be always incomplete guides for teachers.

John Collier

From 1933–1945, John Collier was Commissioner of Indian Affairs. Although that position appears far removed from educational research, much of what he did as Commissioner helped lay the foundation for action research. After decades of the United States government trying to eliminate American Indians' land holdings and culture—and eventually their lives—Collier wrote extensively about the injustices perpetrated on indigenous peoples and the harm the government had imposed. His concern as Commissioner was to find ways to restore dignity to and improve living conditions for the remaining tribes, who were living in poverty and decline after decades of mistreatment. His concern was change and improvement, and he brought a new perspective both to the Bureau and to **social science** research when he took on the job.

Social science
Science exploring the nature of human societies and interactions, including education, sociology, political science, and economics.

One of his chief criticisms—similar to that of teachers who reject one-size-fits-all educational strategies—was that government policies assumed that all tribes were the same. In reality, tribes varied widely: some farmed in the desert without irrigation, and others with it; some specialized in fishing, and others in hunting and trapping; some grazed sheep, and others grazed cattle or reindeer; some believed in laboring to support themselves, and others in renting out their lands and doing as little work as possible. And yet, as Collier objected, "To this boundless diversity our government [has]…for a century—until a few years ago—tried to apply a single formula, one unyielding concept and program" (1945, p. 268). Government policy had been, in other words, the equivalent of prescribing snowsuits for every child.

In contrast, Collier's efforts to find ways to accommodate the diversity of the tribes led him, like Dewey, to argue that social science research needs to be carried out in the complex real world settings where findings are to apply. As Dewey called for teachers to be among those researching practice, Collier called for those who would be affected by the findings to be among those who helped shape them: "[S]ince the findings of the research must be carried into effect by the administrator and the layman, and must be criticized by them through their experience, the administrator and the layman must themselves participate creatively in the research, impelled as it is from their own area of need" (1945, p. 276). Collier's assertion also embeds a second characteristic common to today's action research—that questions are to come from participants' "own area of need" (similar to Dewey's area of "confusion, perplexity, doubt"), a direct contrast to traditional methodology in which experts pose questions. Collier insisted that the surest route to improvement is to allow people who would be affected by change to decide where change is wanted and what action is most likely to effect it—a process he termed "action-research, research-action" (1945, p. 293).

Because education is integrally related to change and quality of life, it is not surprising that one of the several areas where Collier promoted action research projects was education, which he believed needed to be shaped "in terms of live local issues and problems" (1945, p. 274). Ultimately, he became active in the promotion of **progressive** schools, and as Commissioner, he developed collaborative educational research efforts between the Bureau of Indian Affairs and other groups, including the University of Chicago (Collier, 1945; Noffke, 1997). Working with five different tribes, Collier arranged for "a searching study of child development within the context of the community, including the governmental and non-Indian institutions...against the background of the living tribal past and within the web of the natural environment." Although he imagined teams of researchers that would include outside experts, Collier insisted that lay workers and administrators were to be "partners in the research from start to finish" (p. 295). According to Noffke (1997), Collier's "focus on grassroots interest, on collaboration within communities and across disciplines, and on the need for direct links to social action for improvement was a key element

Progressive
an adjective used to describe a set of theorists and practices that define the goal of education as preparing students to become active citizens who promote democratic life.

of this early form of action research" (p. 302). His vision of teams of researchers representing various perspectives (experts as well as members of the community) who work collaboratively together is evident in various strands of today's action research efforts that seek to develop research communities.

In her extensive review of action research literature, Noffke (1997) finds that Collier is one of two figures most often credited with beginning the field of action research, either separately or together. The other is Kurt Lewin, whom one writer terms "the grandfather of action research" (Schmuck, 2006, p. 145).

Kurt Lewin

Like Collier, Lewin was concerned with social issues. As a Jew who emigrated from Germany in 1933 because of widespread discrimination and the rapid rise of Nazism, Lewin was particularly interested in alleviating social prejudice and injustice. And, like Dewey and Collier, he valued basic research, what he referred to as "general laws," but also believed that research needed to move into the real world context: "Research that produces nothing but books will not suffice" (Lewin, 1946, p. 36, 34). His imagery echoes Dewey when he argues that in addition to a knowledge of general laws, the engineer or surgeon "has to know too the specific character of the situation at hand" (p. 37). More specifically, he stressed the need to consider "the inhabitants of that particular main street and those side and end streets which make up the small or large town in which the individual group worker is supposed to do his job" (p. 34). Lewin and his graduate students—many of whom became well known for their own subsequent action research work—completed pioneering studies on intergroup relations not only in business but also in many areas of community life. His description of the action research process is also familiar: "a spiral of steps each of which is composed of a circle of planning, action and fact-finding about the result of the action" (1946, p. 38).

Lewin had a lasting impact on industrial relations because of his work in factories, where he used social science research to counter economic and social discrimination. In one of his best known studies, he demonstrated that untrained female workers hired for factory work, whom managers generally resented and believed could

never perform as well as men, were in fact equally capable. Through an experimental action research process, Lewin demonstrated that all workers could perform at an equally high level if they were trained not in the usual authoritarian and didactic manner, but if groups were given some control over their work and the ability to offer feedback on their training. In this well known work, Lewin not only improved the climate for female workers but also demonstrated the benefit of creating more democratic workplaces. In encouraging participants to systematically collect data to assess situations, Lewin helped many workers and citizens uncover discrepancies between their often-biased beliefs and the reality of a situation.

Among Lewin's greatest talents, says Adelman (1993), was that he could "take contentious social issues and refute the taken-for-granted, often pessimistic assumptions about 'human nature,' and replace these with what has become a new 'common sense'" (p. 9). Lewin's ideas filtered into education, and they were adopted and implemented by the Horace Mann-Lincoln Institute for School Experimentation at Teachers College, Columbia University as well as at the Tavistock Institute in England (Creswell, 2002). They are most evident today in conceptions of action research that involve group work facilitated or supported by an outside expert.

Stephen M. Corey

Most often credited with promoting action research in education, Stephen Corey served as a dean and professor of education at Teachers College as well as executive director of the Horace Mann-Lincoln Institute, which as noted above, was significantly influenced by the ideas of social psychologist Kurt Lewin. From these prestigious positions, he promoted the use of action research for educational improvement and, with his colleagues, emphasized the "knowledge, vitality, and dignity of teachers" (Noffke, 1997, p. 316). As a result, his work is particularly known for having promoted and advanced the professionalism and status of teachers.

The Institute developed a collaborative relationship with schools, doing a great deal of work on curriculum, and it maintained the principle that parents, teachers, students and others of the school community had roles as participants in the research, not simply as passive research subjects (Noffke, 1997). In 1953, after eight years' experience with action research projects nationally, which included extensive work with administrators in the Denver schools (Schmuck, 2006), Corey authored *Action Research to Improve School Practice*. That text is a seminal work whose importance continues to be recognized; It includes six conditions that promote the success of action research efforts that still offer valuable guidance: willingness to admit weakness, opportunity for creativity, opportunity to test ideas, cooperation among administration and staff, systematic data collection, and the time necessary to engage in the reflective process (Schmuck, 2006).

Sensitive to an emerging conception of action research as something less, and less important than, traditional scientific method, Corey offered a vigorous defense, arguing that it is an important and legitimate tool for educators to improve their practice: "The action researcher is interested in the improvement of the educational practices in which he is engaging. He undertakes research in order to find out how to do his job better—action research means research that affects actions" (Corey 1949, p. 509) (in McTaggart, 1991, p. 11). Corey's emphasis on collaboration and on teachers researching elements of their own practice are characteristic of many contemporary action research approaches.

Later On: Renewal in the 1960s and 1970s

Following these prominent early efforts, interest in action research waned for a variety of reasons, including increasing criticism, noted above, that it was not a truly scientific or particularly valuable process. Corey's defense of action research was muted in an environment that included teacher shortages, change in school populations, the Cold War, and McCarthyism; increasingly, it was felt that the issues of curriculum and policy were best left in the hand of experts (Noffke, 1997). Moreover, the federal government began funding educational research, and its criteria for funding appeared to discriminate between researchers and practitioners; action research proposals were often deemed "confused" and fared poorly (Sanford, 1970).

As a result, the focus of action research for those who remained interested shifted from a way to foster large changes in both policy and practice to a means of professional development, especially for teachers. Figures frequently associated with this shift include Hilda Taba and

Abraham Shumsky, who helped moved the "concept of teacher-researcher toward that of teacher-learner" (Noffke, 1997, p. 318). Frequently, outside experts—university professors as a rule—were brought in to facilitate such research. Whereas Corey stressed the professionalism of teachers and the contributions they could make to knowledge in the field, this trend during the middle of the century directed teachers' attention to their own growth—a valuable pursuit, of course, but far more limited than the possibilities imagined by reformers like Lewin and Corey. So thoroughly had the focus changed and the expert resumed the role of researcher that in 1970 an article appeared in *Journal of Social Issues* titled "Whatever Happened to Action Research?" (Sanford, 1970).

However, even as one writer was examining the ghost of early action research work, others were publishing ideas that would give action research new life into the next century. In the 1960s and 70s, new works and leaders again refocused the field, providing contributions that remain seminal to current thinking.

Lawrence Stenhouse

Lawrence Stenhouse, who founded the Center for Applied Research in Education at the University of East Anglia, England in 1970, was a key supporter of teachers as action researchers, echoing earlier champions of action research when he argued "researchers must justify themselves to practitioners, not practitioners to researchers" (1981, p. 113). Stenhouse's 1975 text, *An Introduction to Curriculum Research and Development,* significantly helped revive interest in the idea of teacher-researcher and the ways in which schools and teaching could be improved through systematic self-analysis.

His work is responsible for the widespread growth of action research communities in schools in England and internationally. In 1976 with his colleague John Elliott, Stenhouse founded the Collaborative Action Research Network (CARN), an international group of teachers, administrators and teacher educators involved in action research efforts (Holly et al., 2005). Still an extremely active organization that now includes "members from educational, health, social care, commercial, and public services settings," CARN launched its *Educational Action Research Journal* in 1993 (http://www. did.stu.mmu.ac.uk/

carn/whatis.shtml). Stenhouse's legacy has been in developing and promoting mutually supportive action research communities.

Paulo Freire

While Stenhouse reiterated the need for practitioners to conduct their own research, the work of Brazilian educator Paulo Freire in the last decades of the twentieth century refocused and reenergized some of Collier and Lewin's earlier ideas about using action research as a means to improving social conditions. It is impossible to summarize or adequately capture Freire's importance and influence in educational reform; as Joe Kincheloe has said, "I suppose Paulo Freire is the closest thing education has to a celebrity" (1997, p. vii). His many works have been foundational to current reform efforts world-wide; perhaps the best known and most widely cited is his *Pedagogy of the Oppressed* (1970).

Freire theorized that education is properly a process of learning to "read" the world, and from his perspective, education and social activism are one and the same thing. According to Freire, both the oppressed—those who suffer discrimination—and the oppressors—those whose often unacknowledged privileges come at the expense of others—need to engage in a self-critical process that raises questions about previously unexamined thinking and habits. Only through such self-awareness can people free themselves from unquestioned (and often unconscious) cultural assumptions and make genuinely free choices. Unexamined cultural assumptions (for example, people are poor because they're lazy) are a kind of mental prison that cloud a person's vision. Freire's pedagogy intends to stop people from assuming that things must be as they are: to start questioning what *is* and trying to conceptualize what *might* be.

Freire's work supports action research in that it stressed that those who live a situation must be the ones who analyze it and identify possibilities for action and change; what makes his work seminal is his stress on power relationships and social justice. Those who have adopted Freire's perspective argue for various forms of critical action research (also called emancipatory or liberatory). These models are overtly activist, based on the belief that many education problems are born of social and economic conditions that require change.

Cohesive Threads and Early Tensions

In the work of these early theorists, the patriarchs of the action research family, several features in contemporary action research are evident. All stressed that actions to improve real world conditions—whether tribal living conditions, managerial attitude, worker performance, teacher performance, student achievement, or social inequity—must be informed by the thinking of those to be affected by any resulting change. Thus, every form of action research involves the worker or manager or teacher or student or school or community member to be affected.

Also evident in this brief survey are the several threads that have come together to form different strands of current conceptions. Woven through the work of these various theorists are various emphases on: individuals vs. groups as researchers; promotion of democratic life; the proper relationship between experimental research and field research; the appropriate role of the expert; a focus on improving individuals and/or organizations and/or communities and/or overarching social arrangements. Together, their work responds to questions that remain under discussion:

- What are the appropriate roles for practitioner and expert in generating and using knowledge?
- Does action research produce personally meaningful advice for the practitioner, important feedback to experts, or new knowledge for the field?
- Should action research pursue improvement in individuals, organizations, or societies?

Various answers to these central questions, most often following a path begun by one or more of these early theorists, provide the varied answers to the question "What is action research?"

However, an essential preliminary question is "What counts as research?" Every definition of action research includes assumptions about this core issue, which is a longstanding and exceedingly controversial one. Therefore, before offering more detail on various AR models, Chapter 2 outlines alternative paradigms of scientific research and explains which of these paradigms action research fits within and why.

GLOSSARY

Action research: a process of systematic inquiry, usually cyclical, conducted by those inside a community rather than by outside experts; its goal is to identify action that will generate some improvement the researcher believes important.

Cyclical: an ongoing process in which the same steps are continually repeated.

Critical (emancipatory or liberatory): term/s indicating a concern with unequal power arrangements and a conception of education as activism in the interest of social justice; such work is often significantly grounded in the work of Brazilian educator and theorist Paulo Freire.

Paradigm: a world view; a set of theoretical or philosophical beliefs.

Progressive: an adjective used to describe a set of theorists and practices that define the goal of education as preparing students to become active citizens who promote democratic life.

Social science: Science exploring the nature of human societies and interactions, including education, sociology, political science, and economics.

CHAPTER TWO

Scientific Paradigm and Action Research Models

This chapter explains two different views of research, where action research fits within them, and why, providing a framework for the following discussion of various action research models.

Understanding the Worlds of Scientific Paradigm

In their everyday language, Americans frequently use a color metaphor: "It's not a black or white issue." The implication is that some things are mutually exclusive options—either/or—unable to exist simultaneously. Any attempt to combine them produces a muddle of gray, neither black nor white.

Research paradigms are the equivalent of black or white: the core ideas are so different that they are mutually exclusive. Think, for example, of how the belief that the world was flat affected early explorers. That seminal belief controlled what the explorers believed possible: afraid to sail too far into the horizon for fear they would fall off the edge of the world, they navigated a limited territory strictly bounded by that belief. In contrast, when people began to believe the world was round, an entirely

Paradigm shift

a change in core beliefs that evokes a profound change in how one understands the world. The concept can be traced to Thomas Kuhn's seminal work *The Structure of Scientific Revolutions* (1962).

Positivist

a perspective that defines knowledge as something that exists independently in the world and that can be discovered through careful observation; since it exists independently, knowledge is verifiable and stable.

Interpretivist (constructivist)

a perspective that defines knowledge as dependent upon human perception, and thus as never free from such influences as culture, history, and belief. Because perceptions vary, multiple realities exist simultaneously. Interpretivist research intends to better understand alternative perceptions.

new world of exploration possibilities opened since the perceived danger was eliminated by the new belief. It was never possible, however, to believe the world was round *and* flat. Either it was round and safe to sail, or it was flat with the edge posing a distinct danger. Because so much changed when that core belief shifted, the change could be called a **paradigm shift**: a change in belief so profound as to completely change the way the world and its possibilities are perceived.

The equivalent black/white, round/flat dichotomy in educational research consists of the **positivist** paradigm and the **interpretive** (or **constructivist**) paradigm, two entirely different frameworks with opposing core beliefs. Accepting one or the other expands or limits research possibilities in much the same way as believing the world was flat or round expanded or limited exploration. Although there are many variations of each, all research falls within one of these two paradigms. Therefore, understanding them is a prerequisite to understanding various strands of action research, including how and why they vary, when and why a researcher might adopt this or that definition of *action research,* or what makes it appropriate to use this or that methodology. This chapter first details the two opposing paradigms—positivist and interpretive—and the implications each holds for a researcher's world of possibility. For each, a different core belief about **epistemology**, or knowledge, shapes the world of research possibilities.

The Positivist Paradigm

What is knowledge?

Epistemology

a theory of knowledge, including what knowledge is, where it comes from, and what its limits are.

Natural sciences

science exploring the nature of the physical world— astronomy, geology, biology, chemistry and physics, for example.

When most people use the phrase *scientific research,* they are thinking of research conducted in **natural sciences**, where knowledge constitutes facts discovered through controlled experiments and careful observation. In such fields as chemistry, physics or biology, for example, once research yields a finding, it doesn't change. If oxygen and carbon are combined in certain proportions, the result is carbon monoxide; if combined in specific other proportions, the result is carbon dioxide. If water is heated to a certain temperature, it becomes steam; if cooled to a certain temperature, it becomes ice. Moreover, because results of one researcher must be verified by others before they are accepted as reliable, positivist findings are considered

universal. If such scientific research establishes that water freezes at 32°F, then that will be true in Kansas or New Mexico as well as in Somalia or Italy.

As the social sciences matured as academic disciplines, they generally followed the research lead of the natural sciences, using the same assumptions and methods. Most importantly, positivist social science assumes that it is possible to discover universal truths about human behavior just as natural science discovers truths about the physical world. To uncover these truths, social scientists in the positivist tradition developed experimental and mathematical procedures mirroring those in the natural sciences. For example, psychologists have conducted experiments in which human subjects watched a series of rapidly shifting and contrasting types of pictures (nature scenes interspersed with violent scenes, for example); then, researchers measured the subjects' eye movements from picture to picture as an indicator of whether and how humans respond to different types of images.

Findings in this tradition depend upon direct observation on the positivist assumption that we can only *know* about things we can observe. A **corollary** here is that internal/subjective experience has no place in scientific research. In fact, the positivist stresses that the researcher must be entirely objective and must use methods that can be replicated no matter who or where a specific researcher may be. In the positivist paradigm, any subjective influence would muddy the waters that science seeks to make clear.

For the positivist, then, knowledge consists of discovered truths about the world. Knowledge is fixed, sure, stable; verified; universal; something that exists independently of the researcher. It is a thing, like a nugget of coal or gold, waiting hidden in the world until someone goes to the trouble to find it. From these facts science builds theory to explain them, but to do so it needs reliable and stable facts.

Corollary

a logical inference from an established premise.

Variable

one factor that appears to influence another, so that a change in one correlates with a change in the other. For example, an educational researcher might study whether an increase in nightly homework correlates with higher standardized test scores.

What is the purpose of research? Who conducts it? What use are its findings?

Since truths/facts exist independently in the world, the purpose of positivist research is to discover them. Such discovery depends upon carefully controlling possible influences, or **variables**, in order to identify the relationship of one factor to another. For example, to determine the effec-

tiveness of a particular chemical compound in promoting flower growth, at least two of the same flowering plants, in the same condition, would have to be compared. One plant would get the chemical compound (or treatment), and one wouldn't, while all other conditions—sunshine, water, soil quality—would be kept exactly the same to ensure the chemical treatment and not anything else best correlated to growth differences. Or, in the social sciences, comparable classes might be identified and some taught a concept in a new, experimental way, others in a traditional way; differences in the test scores might be analyzed to assess the effectiveness of the experimental strategy. The job of the scientist is to design experiments that involve controls on the variables, allowing for confidence in linking one specific factor to another. Meticulously controlled experiments also allow other scientists to reproduce an experiment and verify its results.

Because experiments require exactness and rigid control, a high level of sophistication in experimental design and procedure as well as in mathematical calculation is required of researchers, who are experts in their fields and in statistical analysis. Their findings inform the work of practitioners, whose job it is to apply researchers' findings to their own work.

The Interpretive Paradigm

What is knowledge?

FIGURE 2

What makes the interpretive paradigm incompatible with the empirical paradigm is its entirely different definition of knowledge. Most simply stated, where the positivist believes there is a single factual reality waiting to be discovered, the interpretivist believes instead there are multiple realities that vary with the observer. In this paradigm, theorists stress that everything we experience is filtered through our senses, so there is no way to eliminate the human filter and obtain the objectivity that positivists stress. All that anyone can report is his or her *perceptions* of the world, not some independent reality. For example, many readers will have seen Figure 2, which some people see first as a vase and others as two faces. With practice, most people can shift back and forth and learn to see either. This simple illusion demonstrates that the drawing itself has no meaning: it becomes one thing or another

based on what the observer reports seeing, and more than one report—or interpretation—is both possible and credible. The meaning of *vase* or *face* does not independently exist in the drawing but comes instead from the perception of the observer.

From an interpretivist perspective, then, the things of the world have no meaning in and of themselves; all meaning is assigned by human observers. It follows that because every human's perceptions are shaped by personal history, cultures, interests, beliefs, and so on, perceptions of the same event or object will also vary. A person who had never seen a vase or imagined that such an object might exist, for example, would be unable to see a vase in the drawing above. Because no one can escape the influence of experience on perception, the interpretivist rejects the possibility of positivism's strictly objective researcher and single, independent reality.

Of course, interpretivists don't deny facts exist. In the above example, there are black and white shapes that can described in terms of width and angle and so on. However, interpretivists don't view such descriptive information as *knowledge* because it is sterile; that is, it has no meaning in itself. Instead, interpretivists define *knowledge* as the *meaning* people assign to what they observe. From this perspective, knowledge of the drawing consists not of a description of angles and widths, but the meaning an observer assigns to it—vase and/or faces. For obvious reasons, such perceptions are often referred to as *readings* of the world (echoing such other common expressions as "I had a hard time reading his body language"). Since the drawing itself is not inherently one thing or the other, the only thing a researcher can do is seek to understand how various people perceive it, and why.

For this reason, interpretivists say that all knowledge is **socially constructed**: the people in a social group (a culture or a situation or a discipline or a religion or whatever) construct/create and assign meaning (to a gesture or rain or a smile or a vein of carbon) depending upon their particular background of experience. In refuting the idea that the natural sciences, at least, can be objective, interpretivists point out past paradigm shifts even there, where yesterday's truth may be discarded tomorrow—as, for example, when astronomers decided that Pluto was not, after all, a planet. In the above example of the subjects

Socially constructed

a seminal term in interpretivism, which holds that all knowledge is socially constructed. That is, the world consists not of a single independent reality, but instead of multiple realities constructed by people whose perceptions vary with their backgrounds.

exposed to various images, the interpretivist would be far less interested in the fact that eye movement occurred and much more interested in what those movements might mean. That is, were the subjects thrilled, stimulated or appalled by the violent images? While the eye movements might have been the same, the subjects' experiences might have been very different.

What is the purpose of research? Who conducts it?
What use are its findings?

Because there is no single truth to discover, interpretivist research seeks instead to better *understand* (rather than to prove) something. What does this person, or this group, or this culture understand this particular thing to be and to mean? How is that understanding the same as or different from the researcher's or others' perspective? Why? And what are the implications?

In this paradigm, the question of when an exploration becomes *research* is widely debated, which in part accounts for different strands of action research. There is, however, more general agreement on who can benefit from findings, and how. Often, individuals use improved understanding to help design strategies to reach some goal. For example, a teacher who wants students to start doing homework he perceives as important would do well to investigate why students *aren't* doing it. Students who get A's without doing homework might perceive it as pointless busywork, while students who are failing despite their best efforts might perceive it as a frustrating exercise in futility. A different strategy would be called for in each case to better align the meaning that teacher and students assigned to the task. Or, groups can work together in some community (within a school or within a school community, for example) to explore a pervasive problem, like poor student health.

More generally, interpretivist findings can be useful to others when they offer new insights into related situations. For example, when researcher Shirley Brice Heath (1983) published what she learned about how culture affected students' language use in two Appalachian communities, her insights about the importance of understanding students' home culture proved potentially useful to any teacher working with students from a different and unfamiliar background, no matter what the specific background might

be. Interpretivist findings do not provide the prescriptions positivist research seeks but instead offer insights that others can apply to their own situation when they see similarities in context.

An important interpretive sub-category: Critical theory and research

One type of interpretivist research merits its own sub-category. Critical (emancipatory, or liberatory) research is built upon interpretivist epistemology, but it differs substantively from other interpretivist work in that it seeks specific goals. All research described with these terms focuses on unequal power arrangements, and its purpose is to promote social equity. Or, stated more directly, critical work always pursues social justice. It asks who has more power than whom, how they got it, how they maintain it, at what cost to others, and how things might be different.

When critical researchers undertake their own projects, they help to uncover the way privilege works—as, for example, in an analysis of how businesses have become so privileged that they have been able to pollute the environment in poor areas, creating unhealthful conditions for children. Or, they may help relatively powerless groups to analyze their situation, questioning whether things must be the way they are and helping them identify strategies to change things they no longer want to accept. A researcher might work with residents in a poor area, for example, to help them trace their undesirable living conditions back to the privileged role of business in their community and help them think through possibilities for pursuing change. Because critical practitioners always seek more equal power sharing, they sometimes refer to themselves as **cultural workers**, an indication that they consider it their work to promote change in existing, inequitable cultures.

Cultural workers
those who work toward changing existing culture, or society, in the interest of more equal and just power arrangements.

It is important to note, however, that a precept of critical work is that desire and strategy for change must not be prescribed by the researcher but must be developed by working groups of those affected—as Collier argued, for example, when working with native American tribes (see Chapter 1).

Summary of the paradigms and terminology

Table 1 summarizes common terminology associated with each paradigm, although there are shades of meaning in each term that make equating them inaccurate; neverthe-

less, such terms as positivist and empirical are frequently conflated in educational literature. When a writer uses the term *empiricist,* it may often be intended to mean *positivist.*

Different terminologies may indicate some differences in approach, but variations within a paradigm never differ on epistemology. Anyone conducting research in the positivist paradigm intends to discover a fixed external reality, whereas anyone working in the interpretive paradigm intends to better understand multiple possible realities. For the sake of clarity, it is important to note as well that while all critical research is interpretivist, not all interpretivist research is critical.

TABLE 1: TERMINOLOGY ASSOCIATED WITH MAJOR PARADIGMS

	Interpretivist Research	
Positivist Research		**Critical**
Empirical	Naturalistic	Emancipatory
Experimental	Qualitative	Liberatory
Process-Product		
Quantitative		

Epistemological Issues in Educational Research

The difference in epistemology between the positivist and the interpretivist paradigms explains a great deal about major differences in different types of educational research, including action research. Specifically, goals and possibilities of educational research vary between and within paradigms. While the fields are so complex that any general picture will be incomplete or inaccurate in some way, the following broad-brush sketches will offer a serviceable orientation to each.

Positivist educational research

Like other social scientists, many educational researchers have embraced the positivist paradigm and pursued a single, reliable answer to the question "What is the best way to teach?" The positivist school of educational research gave rise to **behaviorism.**, From behaviorism came the idea that all behavior is a response to some stimulus, or prompt; therefore, the goal of research is to identify how

Behaviorism

a type of experimental educational research that seeks to explain human behavior in terms of stimulus-response ("If stimulus *a* is applied, then response *b* will occur"). Mathematical analysis is used to determine correlations between some treatment and a desired response.

Process-product research

research that works to identify relationships between process (what a teacher does) and outcomes (student performances). See also behaviorism.

Quantitative research

depends upon mathematical analysis and often also referred to as *empirical* research. Although this term is frequently used interchangeably with *positivist research*, the only dependable similarity is its reliance on mathematical analysis of data.

Empirical research

depends upon mathematical analysis and so is often referred to as *quantitative* research. Although this term is frequently used interchangeably with *positivist research*, the only dependable similarity is its reliance on mathematical data analysis.

specific stimuli can be used to reliably prompt or discourage specific responses. So, for example, a parent can use the promise of a bedtime story (the stimulus) to get a child to willingly climb into bed (the response). The influence of behaviorism has long been evident in such common classroom practices as placing stickers on good work as a reward (positive reinforcement) and taking away recess as punishment (negative reinforcement).

Believing that universal principles exist, positivist educational researchers work to discover the "one best way" to teach. Of course, no one denies that human emotions and personalities exist, or that they exert influence. However, generally behaviorists believe it is unnecessary—as well as impossible—to research such internal factors. Instead, they focus on identifying particular stimuli that will most reliably produce specific learning outcomes. In this view, researchers determine the "right" way to teach, making teaching simply the act of following scientifically endorsed procedures.

Educational research in the positivist paradigm is known as **process-product research**: which process will best produce the desired product (learning or behavior)? If the teacher follows process *a*, will it result in the product of student behavior *b*? Recognizing that even highly controlled conditions can't possibly eradicate every idiosyncrasy of human behavior, such research tries to identify not absolute causes but mathematical correlations. That is, researchers work to determine how often result *b* appears concurrently with treatment *a*, reasoning that when two things are found together often enough, a relationship between them can be established. Because of its dependence on mathematics, such research is also often referred to as **quantitative** or **empirical research** (though it's important to note that not all work involving mathematics falls into the positivist paradigm). Process-product research is also considered prescriptive, because it offers teachers a prescription for what they should do in their classrooms.

The classical behaviorist view has softened a bit in the recognition of the many combinations of variables that can affect student performance, but the goal of finding reliable rules for teaching remain. Early educational researchers like Dewey who argued for the involvement of teachers in research were not arguing against positivist work itself,

but stressing that findings needed to be tested outside the laboratory and that teachers had to be the ones to decide whether a particular finding applied to a particular situation or not. In short, often objections to behaviorism attack not its method or its findings, but their too-rigid application in the classroom.

There are, however, multitudes of vociferous interpretive researchers who reject any notion of "one best way" to teach, as they reject any idea of a single, independently existing reality to be discovered. Their objections have not changed the fact that the positivist paradigm has been privileged in early twenty-first century legislative educational reform. For example, the **Reading First** grant program promotes "scientific" scripted materials that purport to have captured *the* best way to teach reading and that tell teachers what to say and do every moment of every lesson. Moreover, the political reform movement embedded in **No Child Left Behind** embeds behaviorist principles. That is, it assumes that the stimuli of substantive rewards and punishments based on standardized test scores will be sufficient to prompt all teachers and students to respond by increasing scores on mandated tests.

Reading First

a grant program to provide money for the teaching of reading in American schools. Grants were awarded only to schools that adopted highly structured (scripted) reading materials from a few publishers that the administration favors as being "scientific."

What does this mean for action researchers?

Simply stated, action research—because it is always context specific, focused on a specific situation—does not fit within the positivist research paradigm. It seeks local, rather than universal, understandings and strategies. Unfortunately, many curious educators familiar only with the positivist paradigm may turn away from systematic research because they lack training in statistical procedures, or they realize they cannot work with the large numbers that positivist research requires; that is, they may feel constrained by methods and standards that simply do not and cannot apply to action research. Or perhaps worse, they may attempt research anyway and end up producing the kind of muddle mentioned above: a contextual study that illogically and impossibly tries in convoluted ways to mimic the rigid requirements of positivist research.

No Child Left Behind

legislation that requires, among other things, that students regularly take standardized tests with substantive penalties or rewards depending on student scores. Because consequences can have lifelong effects for students, educators and schools, the plan is known as *high-stakes testing.*

Educators need neither refrain from systematic inquiry nor entangle themselves in sterile attempts to "prove" something definitively. An understanding of the interpretive paradigm makes clear that it is a hospitable home for action research. Moreover, a researcher who is clear on

the purpose and paradigm of a particular study can even use generic positivist methodologies (experimental design, statistical analysis) for interpretive purposes. The essential difference to keep in mind is that the positivist seeks truth while the interpretivist seeks understanding.

Interpretivist educational research

Interpretivists, who believe that not one reality but multiple realities exist, offer a wide range of objections and alternatives to educational research as a source of prescriptions for teachers. However, it is important to note at the beginning of this discussion that few interpretivists would argue for eliminating positivist research. There is little doubt that it has produced many general observations that are useful to practitioners. For example, such research helped make teachers aware of how little time they generally gave students to think about a question before answering it; consequently, many teachers have adopted minimal "wait time" guidelines and begun getting more and better answers to their questions. Interpretivists generally acknowledge that work in the positivist paradigm can provide useful food for thought; however, they reject any idea that there exists one best way of teaching appropriate for all students in all situations. The positivist view, from an interpretive perspective, is just one more of many possible ways of reading the world.

Interpretivist research has very different goals than positivists. Rather than discovering universals, it seeks to understand the multiple realities that co-exist in a specific educational context. For example, if a school were suffering from daily episodes of student violence, an interpretivist researcher might try to understand what students perceived as existing student social groups, how each group defined or characterized other groups, which students identified with which groups, what incompatible values or understandings were generating conflict, and whether students themselves saw any alternatives to violence as a means of resolving conflicts. Interpretivists believe that understanding the multiple perspectives of stakeholders involved in a situation is a prerequisite to designing strategies for improvement.

Interpretivists generally share their new understanding with others, those involved in the situation and often with outsiders as well, in the hope that new information on

competing perspectives will help effect desirable change. Of course, no interpretivist would expect that findings in one situation would automatically apply to another; a school divided by race is not the same as a school divided by competing gangs. However, the interpretivist researcher often shares his or her work in the hope that a context-specific study might nevertheless provide others dealing with a similar problem some ideas about potentially useful methodologies, strategies and insights. It remains always the educator's responsibility, however, to decide when, where, and *if* findings of *any* research, interpretivist or positivist, provide useful insight.

The goal of interpretivist educational research is to foster a deep understanding of specific situations among various stakeholders who can then better align goals and strategies with the multiple perspectives shaping the issue.

An important distinction: Epistemology vs. methodology

Not surprisingly, the methods of positivism and interpretivism are very different. As already noted, positivists depend on mathematical analysis that allows them to predict with a high degree of probability that two variables will correlate—that they will always or nearly always appear together (suggesting, but not proving, cause and effect). For example, a positivist study might examine how use of a certain text correlates with high test scores, implying a relationship between the text and performance. In such research, **data** and findings are numbers—for example, frequency rates ("Students in this class have typically failed x out of y exams"), or ranges ("The highest score differed from the lowest by 72 points"), or raw scores ("The highest failing score was 53, the lowest 6").

Data

information; in research, the information analyzed to answer the research question.

Interpretivist methods are very different. Because researchers are trying to understand how others see the world, they rely on a variety of ways to make others' internal thoughts and beliefs external. For example, interviews are common as a way to extract a subject's thinking and perceptions. Interviews can be one-on-one or in the form of focus groups, where people are brought together to provide their thinking on a specific issue. Or written documents, like diaries, can be examined. Because it's difficult for a researcher to be sure how reliable any one source is, most often methods are combined—interviews with a variety of people, observation of various people and activities, and surveys might all be combined as different "lenses" on the same subject. Later chapters will offer more detail on interpretivist methodology, but the major point here is that almost anything that may offer insight about a person or thing can be a source of information, or data, in this paradigm.

A critical caveat about methodology: The most important point to remember about methodology is that either type of methodology can be used in a particular research study in either paradigm. As researchers have increasingly recognized the advantages and limitations of each paradigm and methodology, "mixed-method" studies are becoming more common. To return to the example above, a process-product researcher might want to determine which variables correlate most strongly with student test failure. However, such research can't begin until the researcher has some ideas about possible variables. Rather than simply making an informed guess, the researcher might spend some time interviewing failing students (an interpretive methodology) to see what they suggest as possibilities. Thus, preliminary interpretive work can help a researcher identify variables to manipulate in a correlational (quantitative) study.

Conversely, a teacher might have the sense that his classes are going well but might want to double check to be sure that all students are performing within reasonable bounds. So, he might lay out a grid of test scores and note that there are only two F's, which doesn't seem unusual. In the past, students failing at one point in a semester were often just a little behind and normally caught up by the end of the marking period. Just to be sure, this teacher might look a little deeper, at the specific raw scores, and find that both students have raw averages 40 points lower than the lowest C student. Moreover, both had actually begun the marking period with passing grades. In this case, doing even this simplistic statistical analysis might uncover an area that cries out for additional, interpretive investigation in order to *understand* the students' performance and help them improve. In other words, a look at quantitative data can suggest an area where a qualitative study might be useful.

Generally, then, methodology typical of one paradigm can be used to inform efforts in the other. What is

most important is to keep the difference in goals between paradigms in mind to avoid producing results that are a muddled mixture of black and white. A researcher who isn't clear on different purposes of research is likely to mismatch methods with purpose and ultimately produce a study that neither paradigm finds credible.

Summary

Positivist research seeks reliable truths and dependable universal generalizations; in contrast, interpretivist research seeks understanding of the multiple realities that exist in any situation. Because educational action research always begins with a local question and explores a local context, seeking local rather than global insight, by definition it falls into the interpretive paradigm. Nevertheless, an action research project may employ either positivist (quantitative) or interpretivist (qualitative, or constructivist) methodologies—or both—in an effort to develop deeper understanding of a local context.

Despite the fact that action research studies fall within the interpretive paradigm, there is great variation among them. The following section explores the many choices that researchers make when designing a study.

Variables in Action Research Models

As noted in Chapter 1, the term *action research* describes not a single practice but a "large family" of "beliefs and relationships" (Noffke, 1997, p. 306). To differentiate among these, various theorists and researchers have generated a wide variety of terms. A few are fairly well established. For example, educational **participatory action research** is widely understood to refer to research that involves multiple stakeholders and intends to change not only schools but society at large. However, there is far more deviance than agreement in terminology: two different terms may be used for essentially the same thing, or the same term may mean different things to different people. For example, the terms **teacher research** and **teacher inquiry** are far less exact, though both stress that the teacher is the one who does the work.

Because terminology is so fluid, various strands of action research are not easily or reliably named and categorized. To avoid unproductive terminology tangles, instead of offering categories this discussion explores some key

---

Participatory action research

research by groups pursuing the emancipatory (critical/ liberatory) goal of a more democratic and just society. Multiple stakeholders work together democratically to address problems rooted in social conditions that they seek to change. Problems/ issues are named by those who directly experience them.

Teacher inquiry/ Teacher research

Catch-all, ill-defined terms used to refer to multiple models of educational action research; either term's meaning in a specific context depends upon the purposes and processes of the model.

questions that lead to significant variations among models. Where there is widespread agreement on a term, it will be included—but understanding rather than terminology remains the focus here.

Newcomers to action research would do well to remember that because conflicting models co-exist, there is no "right" way to undertake action research. The practitioner who decides to undertake a project can chart his or her own path by choosing among the alternatives discussed below. It is not unusual for practitioners to begin with a modest, practical action research goal and, over time, to develop an interest in much larger questions and projects, often with social and/or political dimensions. Stringer (2004) aptly notes: "As they participate in action research, people develop high degrees of motivation and are often empowered to work in ways they never thought possible" (p. 31).

Two core questions that primarily shape various models are: Who participates in action research? For what purpose/s? The following sections detail possible answers to each. Afterward, a closing discussion offers a closer look at how easily boundaries between models may blur. Projects begun alone can soon lead to collaborative work; projects begun for one purpose can easily end with another. In fact, the most striking feature of action research may be its malleability.

Practitioner researchers must determine their own first commitments, since their interests are properly the core of any action research project. Their choices may be easier, however, if they remember that any beginning path can easily change direction. The general fluidity of the action research concept means that a modest first step may lead to a more ambitious project later.

Who Conducts Educational Action Research?

The key criterion that distinguishes action research from other types of research is that there is *always* someone directly involved in the situation who serves as researcher. A nice description of the distinction comes from Cochran-Smith and Lytle (1993). They differentiate between *research on teaching,* where questions come from earlier research and outside experts, and *teacher research,* where the practitioner formulates questions based on his or her experience and interests. To qualify as action research, at least one stakeholder—teacher, principal, staff member—must be

engaged in finding the answer to some question he or she deems important. For example, a teacher might systematically gather information on a struggling student (class work, daily journal entries on the student's performance, interviews with parents and other teachers) in order to better understand the student's behavior and to devise a plan to improve it. Or, an assistant principal might check for unconscious bias in her disciplinary actions by reviewing records and interviewing students to determine whether punishments have been equitable, or perceived as equitable, in recent months.

While participant involvement is a necessary component, it alone is not sufficient to qualify a particular project as *action research*. Various models differ on who may, or must, be involved, giving rise to the following sub-questions: If only a single stakeholder is involved, can the project properly be called action research? Or, is some group necessary to support the effort? Must an "expert" facilitator be involved? *May* an "expert" facilitator be involved?

Is action research an individual or collective effort?

Many proponents of action research advocate a model in which a single practitioner carries out a project of personal interest and significance. While a researcher can always choose to discuss a project informally with others, sharing information on the experience isn't necessary. The work meets its purpose when an individual researcher devises and implements an effective action plan to improve a problem area. As Hubbard and Power (1999) note, "There are examples of teacher-researchers doing fine studies without support" (p. 6). However, they also add immediately, "usually sustained inquiry in schools or districts over time involves the development of a research community." Whether such a community is necessary or simply desirable is open to debate.

Because unshared, individual work has impact on only one practitioner, some critics argue that it is not truly action research, although it can certainly be useful in improving practice. Such critics argue that to qualify as *research*, the work must have the potential to contribute to the wider field of educational theory and practice— that is, to be useful outside a single classroom. If the lone researcher planned to share findings in some public way

so that others could critique and/or learn from them, then the work would move closer to the definition of research (something that produces new understandings/information useful to others) that many theorists adopt. Such sharing needn't be formal, like a published article; it might include presenting the work to an action research group, or perhaps giving a talk to colleagues during an in-service day. Many theorists would insist anything called action research must have some such sharing component.

Another argument against the model of the lone researcher working in isolation is the need for **trustworthiness**, a proposed standard for judging the quality of action research. Essentially, trustworthiness refers to how credible an audience finds a study based on such factors as whether the data came from multiple sources and whether it included the perspectives of varied stakeholders.

Trustworthiness

a quality standard for interpretive action research which refers to how credible an audience may find a particular study, based on such factors as whether the amount and type of data collected seem appropriate.

> The basic issue in relation to trustworthiness is simple: How can an inquirer persuade his or her audiences (including self) that the findings of an inquiry are worth paying attention to, worth taking account of? What arguments can be mounted, what criteria invoked, what questions asked, that would be persuasive on this issue? (Lincoln & Guba, 1985, 290)

Trustworthiness has been promoted, and increasingly accepted, as a quality standard for interpretive research by theorists who reject empirical standards for interpretive work but argue that some quality standards are essential.

The issue of quality is important to the future of action research, which has been criticized for producing weak and idiosyncratic work. The concept of trustworthiness helps to make clear that while interpretive work presumes the existence of multiple realities, that assumption emphatically does *not* mean that all interpretive studies are equally well researched or well documented. Research projects can be more or less thorough; researchers have unique biases and perspectives that can be more or less accounted for in a study. Some theorists urge that action research should be done in groups at least in part because of quality concerns: a researcher working alone has less chance of seeing weaknesses in a project than one who routinely consults with a group.

Collaborative action research

generally refers to research conducted by stakeholder groups to solve problems in an institution or community. Such projects typically have a practical orientation.

For these and other reasons, many theorists promote some version of **collaborative action research**, which involves a group of researchers working together. Such

groups provide the "peer review, commentary and critique" that strengthen both the research itself and the growth of the practitioner (Clarke & Erickson, 2003, p. 28). Some variation also exists within this model. Groups of teachers from different schools may choose to form an action research group as a kind of support group, where members can offer suggestions and feedback to help improve each other's individual projects. In this case, the researcher still focuses primarily on the world of his or her own classroom. Alternatively, a group of teachers from the same building might decide to explore the same question in their multiple classrooms. For example, if absenteeism were a school-wide problem, then every teacher might learn as much as possible about his or her own students' behavior, with the group coming together to look for school-wide patterns and to devise school-wide strategies to alleviate the problem. Many action research models promote such school-based groups, emphasizing improvements to the school community rather than to individual classrooms.

In still other models and contexts, a cross-community group may come together to work on a school-wide issue such as high absenteeism. In such models, stakeholders view the school as part of a complex social system that must be considered as a whole. Therefore, groups include representatives from outside the school as well as within it, typically including administrators, parents, students, guidance counselors, social workers, law enforcement officers, and so on.

Because collaboration always involves sharing of findings and discussion of their possible application to other classroom and situations, the word *research* to describe collaborative work is more readily accepted.

Must—may—an expert be involved?

Some conceptions of action research call for the involvement of an expert, most often a university professor or other authority (an administrator with research training, for example). The rationale is that the average practitioner has little or no knowledge of the action research process. Therefore, an experienced facilitator is necessary as a guide. Some models explicitly endorse the possibility of this role being filled by experienced peers who can guide colleagues through the process, facilitate supportive group meetings, and handle administrative tasks (for example,

Mohr et al., 2004). In practice, however, university faculty members often serve as expert facilitators. Action research is frequently introduced in university courses for both preservice and inservice teachers, where faculty naturally serve as resident experts. And increasingly, as schools embrace action research as a way of improving practice, districts are inviting university faculty to facilitate action research efforts as ongoing professional development for their teachers.

Some critics worry, however, that models calling for an expert facilitator can undermine what they see as the heart of the action research process—moving power into the hands of practitioners. Crucial power issues are inherent in the divide between empiricism and interpretivism detailed above. Within the empiricist paradigm that has historically dominated education, the expert researcher with specialized training is the only one who can conduct research and identify reliable teaching strategies. This arrangement places the researcher in a more powerful position than the practitioner, whose role is to accept direction from the expert. Action research can disrupt this traditional relationship. As interpretive work that specifically invites practitioners and other stakeholders into the research process, action research authorizes practitioners to identify knowledge for themselves and for their peers. Thus, practitioners assume a role and a power that only outside experts previously enjoyed (Kincheloe, 1991).

Those who understand, and welcome, this change in power arrangements tend to be suspicious of calls for expert involvement. They charge that calls for expert facilitators are a way for those who have long held power over the field—primarily university researchers—to keep their influence over practitioners, as well as their own prestige, in place. Perhaps not coincidentally, any power relationship that keeps practitioners dependent on outside authorities also leads to textbooks and classroom materials being designed outside the classroom as well—a boon for corporations (and expert authors) that produce one-size-fits-all textbooks for teachers to follow.

A similar concern arises for models that propose having administrators lead school- or district-based research groups, even though they are insiders. Because administrators have more power than teachers, they are likely to have significant influence over the research questions asked

as well as other elements of the research process. Critics charge that such models also co-opt the action research process, keeping power in the hands of authorities while appearing to transfer it to teachers. Obviously, contextual factors (the working relationships of participants, for example) will affect how any model functions in a particular location; therefore, in actual practice, involving an expert may prove to be either useful or harmful depending on the specific people involved.

The reality is that practitioners often do not in fact have relevant knowledge and skills for conducting action research. Therefore, even theorists who worry about expert involvement frequently support models that include it. Their strategy is to allow for possible need, *but* to insist that the facilitator take a specific and highly restricted role, supporting—but not shaping—the efforts of others (Carr & Kemmis, 1986). That is, all decisions about research questions, purpose and methods lie solely in the hands of the practitioner-researchers. The facilitator's goal is to provide information and illuminate issues, not to make decisions *for* the researcher/s.

Summary

Any action research project embeds choices about working individually or in a group, and every group reflects some choice about whether an experienced facilitator—either an outside expert or an experienced colleague—is necessary. A practitioner who wants to work alone can select any one of a number of "how-go" guides to action research and become familiar with the typical process (see list of textbooks in the References section as well as later chapters). An intelligent adult can learn to do many things by reading and experimenting. However, many beginners will prefer having an experienced mentor or facilitator, so that a first foray into action research might be involve taking a course or joining an existing research group—or even becoming part of an online community.

What Is the Purpose of Action Research?

As is true for other areas, precision is difficult in a discussion of the purposes of action research because terminology and practice are so variable. There is some agreement that purposes fall into one of two general categories: practical or emancipatory (Carr & Kemmis, 1986;

McTaggart, 1991).[1] However, the terms *critical* or *liberatory* are also frequently used to describe *emancipatory* work. Moreover, the dividing wall between practical and emancipatory research is permeable: edges of each terrain may blur and overlap, as the final section will discuss.

Practical Action Research

Practical action research

research that focuses on improving practice. Typically, a practitioner or group of practitioners identifies a classroom problem and methodically works toward identifying and implementing a specific change strategy.

Practical action research is a process in which practitioners identify a local, practical problem they want to address and then systematically work to identify action strategies for improvement. It may include, but is not limited to, exploring technique. When it does explore technique, its purpose is not to test empirical generalizations (although they may be one type of information considered) but to help practitioners use their own intelligence and creativity to find ways to effect change. Practical action research can be undertaken by single practitioners or by groups, working with or without expert facilitation. When an expert is involved, his or her role is generally "Socratic: to provide a sounding-board against which practitioners may try out ideas and learn more about the reasons for their own action, as well as learning more about the process of self-reflection" (Carr & Kemmis, 1986, p. 203). Obviously, these parameters are so broad that many kinds of projects can fall under the practical action research umbrella: studies of single students or groups of students, of curriculum, of school climate, of support services—anything that can pose a practical obstacle for the educator.

Craft knowledge

what teachers know about teaching based on their classroom experiences; it stands in contrast to empirical ("scientific") findings and is often referred to as *lore* by those who reject it as a legitimate knowledge base.

Theorists who don't believe that the empirical "one best way" to teach can ever be developed often see practical action research as a way to develop a valuable body of knowledge born of practitioner experience—sometimes referred to as **craft knowledge.** Instead of routinely relying on instinct and casual observation, the practical action researcher consciously identifies a concern, considers various potential data sources, collects data systematically, analyzes it carefully, and produces an action plan to improve the original situation. The knowledge born of such a careful reflective process is far more detailed and grounded than a teacher's catch-all of daily reflection. Thus, such research can help capture and solidify much of what teachers know but are too rarely given credit for knowing. While the obvious purpose of practical action research is to improve some condition, many theorists also value its potential to

help practitioners gain more control of practice, to change what counts as "knowledge" of teaching practice, and to help build a body of craft knowledge.

A good example of the potential of an individual practical action researcher to produce such important results is Nancie Atwell's classic text in literacy education, *In the Middle* (1987). As the field of literacy instruction moved away from teaching literature and writing as discrete subjects and toward helping students mature as readers and writers, Atwell's detailed depiction of her classroom workshops provided countless literacy teachers insight into how workshops might be structured, what kinds of lessons students could learn in them, and how ambitious a teacher might be on her students' behalf. While the text presents Atwell's personal experiences, many teachers have found her insights and routines relevant to their own classrooms. There's no doubt that the book had a significant impact on countless other practitioners, producing the kind of improved practice that many theorists hope for from the practical action research process. Atwell's classroom is also a democratic one, and so her work additionally reflects the interests of many theorists who hope to transform the role of teacher from expert transmitter of knowledge to the most experienced learner in a community of learners.

Generally, those who conceptualize teachers as reflective practitioners (Schön, 1983) promote practical action research for professional development and/or as an integral part of lifelong teaching practice. Those who support this model often believe practical action research should be part of undergraduate and graduate coursework, where students may learn to work in groups to support and critique each other's efforts. Many teacher educators hope that such coursework will encourage students to consider self-critique an integral part of practice and perhaps even to promote action research groups in their school communities.

A typical example of practical action research as a university-led form of professional development and school improvement is the Center for School Improvement at the University of Florida (http://education.ufl.edu/web/index.php?pid=903). Its home page states its dedication to helping schools improve by promoting "practitioner inquiry." The Center's director and several of its staff are UFL faculty who design and offer inquiry workshops, providing the expert university support many believe necessary;

however, Center staff also work with a corps of teachers who serve as peer facilitators in their own schools, so that leadership expertise is cultivated among practitioners. The Center sponsors an annual conference, or "showcase," where teachers from across the state can share their work and change strategies.

Many applaud such university-school collaboration and the potential of practical action research to improve and democratize practice. However, some critics argue that a focus on the practical is too shortsighted. They promote instead the more ambitious goals of emancipatory research, which seeks to reform not only schools but also the society that shapes them. For some theorists with this perspective, practical research provides an accessible entry for those new to action research—but more important is its potential as a "stepping-stone" to emancipatory work (Carr & Kemmis, 1986, p. 203).

Emancipatory Action Research

Emancipatory (critical, or liberatory) action research
pursues a more democratic and just society; stresses that educational problems often reflect larger social, political and economic conditions. Emancipatory research stresses questioning why things are as they and how they might be different.

Emancipatory action research, like much other work referred to as *emancipatory, liberatory,* or *critical,* has roots in the work of Brazilian theorist Paulo Freire, especially his well-known *Pedagogy of the Oppressed* (1970). As its name suggests, emancipatory action research is inherently about freedom. More specifically, it is about freeing people from limitations they've unconsciously accepted because they aren't in the habit of asking if things *must* be the way they are. So, for example, teachers may unquestioningly follow a standardized school curriculum because they simply accept it as an unchangeable element of their situations. They aren't in the habit of asking, for example, whether it is the best curriculum for their particular students, or whether administrators and legislators have an inalienable right to impose it. In contrast to such passive acceptance, emancipatory researchers stress the need to question every element of a situation, specifically including conditions they have formerly taken for granted. Inevitably, questions arise about who has power over whom, how they use that power, and to whose benefit and detriment. Conspicuously absent from the emancipatory perspective is an assumption that an educational problem can most often be solved simply by changing an educator's practice.

Contrasting examples of practical and emancipatory action research can help illustrate the difference here. A

teacher whose students year after year fail tests based on a particular math book might conduct *practical* action research to find ways to supplement the text so that student scores improve. The teacher accepts the text as a given in the situation and works to find new practices that will improve outcomes. In contrast, a teacher conducting *emancipatory* action research might ask instead why a text that ill-serves particular students continues to be forced on them—and who selected the text—and why—and who determined the curriculum in the first place—and why—and how things might be different and better for students. Does the current curriculum seem to disadvantage a particular group of students? Which ones? Why? How can the inequity be remedied? The researcher would certainly consult students, because emancipatory action research is a democratic process that stresses giving voice to those affected by decisions. The emancipatory perspective is that most often, poor conditions result from unequal power arrangements distant from, but nevertheless reflected in, classrooms. To change those conditions, multiple stakeholders with different perspectives must work together.

For example, the teacher in the example above might try to initiate an action research group representing administrators, curricular leaders, teachers, students, parents, and any other groups that might have a stake in student success. The group would probe the problem from multiple angles and devise an improvement strategy. At the end of the process, the text—and/or many other things like the curriculum, support services, textbook selection procedures, or teacher assignments—might change, affecting not just one classroom but the entire school and possibly the community beyond. Perhaps there is a need for after-school tutoring, or for a bilingual teacher, that has not been funded. Perhaps teachers are excluded from textbook selection. Perhaps teachers without credentials in teaching math are routinely assigned to teach it. Any of these possibilities hints at systemic bias against certain students (and/or teachers), a problem of concern to an entire community that believes it is supporting public schools where all children have equal opportunity to learn.

Ultimately, emancipatory researchers hope that change begun in the school will help bring change to the community and world beyond the classroom. Schools cannot help but reflect the society in which they exist. They embody

expectations and limitations imposed by a variety of social agents—including politicians, parents, corporations, and others. Given the extent of outside influence, solutions to educational problems are often linked to needed change in social and economic conditions. For example, a child who isn't getting enough food will be distracted by hunger and unable to concentrate no matter which textbook a teacher might use. Hunger is an issue of government policy, which has not adequately addressed the fact that nearly one in five children in the United States (17% in 2005) lives in a family whose income falls below its poverty threshold (ChildStats. gov). Or, students with consistently failing math scores might not be native English speakers, so that they are disadvantaged by laws mandating English-only instruction. Emancipatory researchers never lose sight of the fact that social factors have enormous influence over individual teachers, classrooms, and schools.

Because emancipatory action research's explicit purpose is greater equity, it poses a threat to existing power arrangements. Not surprisingly, such work has its opponents.

> [A]ction researchers...represent a challenge to established authority, and frequently meet resistance at the classroom –level, and the school level and from administrative authorities beyond the school, such as examination boards and educational departments and from communities who expect education today to be like education in previous times. (Carr & Kemmis, 1986, 206)

There is good reason for those in privileged positions to resist (and possibly attempt to co-opt) emancipatory research. Because the existing system benefits them, they prefer to keep today's education "like education in previous times"—in direct contrast to the emancipatory goal of greater equity. Wealthy parents are unlikely to embrace the idea that their children might receive less of a district's resources so that poor children can receive more; administrators who enjoy the simplicity of choosing texts for teachers might not welcome a messy, democratic selection process. Researchers who work in this area can expect to encounter resistance.

Despite such resistance, emancipatory action research has both a strong history and strong supporters and centers. Notably, these include the Deakin University Action Research Group in Australia, and in England, the

University of Bath's resource site, ActionResearch.net. The Deakin group (more specifically, R. McTaggart) has promoted the widely recognized term participatory action research (PAR) to distinguish emancipatory action research from more practical collaborative work. At Bath, both Jack Whitehead and Jean McNiff, who has followed in his footsteps, have promoted a form of educational emancipatory action research that stresses aligning practice with values, "often referred to in terms such as freedom, justice, democracy" (Whitehead, 1989, Section 3, ¶1). Researchers and theorists associated with these institutions have produced a great deal of writing that has clarified and advanced the field.

A good example of long-term participatory action research to address such community issues as affordable housing and access to employment is the East St. Louis Action Research Project (ESLARP), facilitated by College of Fine and Applied Arts, University of Illinois at Urbana-Champaign (http://www.eslarp.uiuc.edu/). The ESLARP website describes its mission as a collaboration among faculty, students, and neighborhood groups in East St. Louis "on highly tangible and visible projects that address the immediate and long-term needs of some of the city's most distressed communities." Representatives of government and other relevant groups are often enlisted to help on projects, which have included building a playground for young children and establishing a vocational education program for high school dropouts. Still more ambitious projects as realizing more affordable housing are described on the ESLARP website.

Summary

Three categories for action research have been formulated by theorists, but only two are widely accepted. *Technical action research,* in which practitioners experiment with recommendations from experts outside the classroom, is often rejected as essentially empiricist and as a way to keep teachers subordinate to researchers. *Practical action research,* in which practitioners explore practical problems and design action strategies to remedy them, is often promoted as a means of improving practice, providing meaningful professional development, and effecting school reform. *Emancipatory action research,* in which educators join with multiple stakeholders in a social community to

identify and address inequities, is promoted by many who argue that because schools are profoundly influenced by social conditions, those conditions must be examined and considered as part of meaningful educational reform.

The Bridge Between Practical and Emancipatory Action Research

While categories can be useful in establishing general understandings about trends in action research, boundaries are often unclear, as already noted. A good example of why categorization is difficult and how one type of project so often leads to another, as the "stepping-stone" metaphor for practical research suggests, is found in the work of Cochran-Smith and Lytle (1993; 1999). Their work has primarily focused on the benefits of action research as a means of improving not only teaching practice but also its culture—and with it the culture of higher and teacher education. Table 2 summarizes the thinking they laid out in their important work *Inside/Outside* (1993).

TABLE 2: SUMMARY OF COCHRAN-SMITH & LYTLE'S VIEW OF TEACHER RESEARCH	
Teacher research: a form of social change wherein individuals and groups labor to understand and alter classrooms, schools, and school communities.*	
Because it challenges traditional assumptions about knowers, knowing, and what can be known about teaching . . .	. . . it can transform the idea of a knowledge base for teaching and challenge the role of university researcher as expert.
Because it challenges the dominant views of teacher education and professional development as the importing of knowledge from outside schools . . .	. . . it can redefine teacher development to make inquiry and reform activities intrinsic to teaching throughout a professional life.
Because it uncovers the ways in which teachers and students co-construct knowledge and curriculum . . .	. . . it can profoundly change teachers' uses of language and literacy and can support a more critical and democratic pedagogy.
*Table content quoted or paraphrased from Inside/Outside (1993, p. xiv)	

Much of this thinking reflects a concern with the development of a body of craft knowledge, typical of the practical orientation: the need for teachers to incorporate inquiry into their daily practice; the idea that practitioners

can uniquely contribute to a knowledge base for teaching; the argument that inquiry is a powerful tool for building powerful curricula. There are, however, also clear emancipatory implications to this thinking. Potential shifts of power, for example, are always of concern in emancipatory work. Other emphases that fit into the emancipatory framework include the idea that not just classrooms but also the larger worlds of schools and school communities might be changed and the belief that action research can lead teachers to more critical (emancipatory) and democratic pedagogy.

Thus, with emphasis on the practical but also with significant attention to emancipatory possibilities, the work of Cochran-Smith and Lytle illustrates that as practical research seeps beyond single classroom walls to change larger communities, it bridges to emancipatory work. The teacher who tries to find ways to supplement a textbook may soon realize that the problem is not her practice but the curriculum, or a lack of support services, or state language policy, and that solutions lie outside the classroom, in conditions shaped by more powerful others. Cochran-Smith and Lytle note the possibility themselves, although they do not use the terms *emancipatory* or *critical* to identify it:

> The concept of teacher as researcher... [can] provide ways to link teaching and curriculum to wider political and social issues. When this happens, teacher research creates dissonance, often calling attention to the constraints of hierarchical arrangements of schools and universities as well as to the contradictions of imperatives for both excellence and equity. This kind of dissonance is not only inevitable, it is also healthy and necessary for change to occur. (1999, p. 22)

It's a short step from asking "How can I alleviate this child's hunger so she can study?" to "Why is this child hungry in the first place?"

Thus, boundaries between these two categories are unstable, and there is no need for action research novices to be able to name this-or-that theorist definitively as a proponent of this-or-that type of action research. What *is* important instead is that they have a general understanding of the possibilities and potential of different approaches. Such understanding will allow them to be more clear-headed and definitive in designing their own projects and to accept

modest starting points, knowing that larger possibilities are likely just down the road.

GLOSSARY

Behaviorism: a type of experimental educational research that seeks to explain human behavior in terms of stimulus-response ("If stimulus a is applied, then response b will occur"). Mathematical analysis is used to determine correlations between some treatment and a desired response.

Collaborative action research: generally refers to research conducted by stakeholder groups to solve problems in an institution or community. Such projects typically have a practical orientation.

Corollary: a logical inference from an established premise.

Craft knowledge: what teachers know about teaching based on their classroom experiences; it stands in contrast to empirical ("scientific") findings and is often referred to as *lore* by those who reject it as a legitimate knowledge base.

Cultural workers: those who work toward changing existing culture, or society, in the interest of more equal and just power arrangements.

Data: information; in research, the information analyzed to answer the research question.

Emancipatory (critical, or liberatory) action research: pursues a more democratic and just society; stresses that educational problems often reflect larger social, political and economic conditions. Emancipatory research stresses questioning why things are as they are and how they might be different.

Empirical research: depends upon mathematical analysis and so is often referred to as *quantitative* research. Although this term is frequently used interchangeably with *positivist research*, the only dependable similarity is its reliance on mathematical data analysis.

Epistemology: a theory of knowledge, including what knowledge is, where it comes from, and what its limits are.

Focus groups: an interpretive method for gathering information. Groups of people are brought together for questioning and conversation with researchers who want to understand their thinking.

Interpretivist (constructivist): a perspective that defines knowledge as dependent upon human perception, and thus as never free from such influences as culture, history, and belief. Because perceptions vary, multiple realities exist simultane-

ously. Interpretivist research intends to better understand alternative perceptions.

Natural sciences: science exploring the nature of the physical world—astronomy, geology, biology, chemistry and physics, for example.

No Child Left Behind: legislation that requires, among other things, that students regularly take standardized tests with substantive penalties or rewards depending on student scores. Because consequences can have lifelong effects for students, educators and schools, the plan is known as *high-stakes testing*.

Paradigm shift: a change in core beliefs that evokes a profound change in how one understands the world. The concept can be traced to Thomas Kuhn's seminal work *The Structure of Scientific Revolutions* (1962).

Participatory action research: research by groups pursuing the emancipatory (critical/liberatory) goal of a more democratic and just society. Multiple stakeholders work together democratically to address problems rooted in social conditions that they seek to change. Problems/issues are named by those who directly experience them.

Practical action research: research that focuses on improving practice. Typically, a practitioner or group of practitioners identifies a classroom problem and methodically works toward identifying and implementing a specific change strategy.

Positivist: a perspective that defines knowledge as something that exists independently in the world and that can be discovered through careful observation; since it exists independently, knowledge is verifiable and stable.

Process-product research: research that works to identify relationships between process (what a teacher does) and outcomes (student performances). See also behaviorism.

Quantitative research: depends upon mathematical analysis and often also referred to as *empirical* research. Although this term is frequently used interchangeably with *positivist research,* the only dependable similarity is its reliance on mathematical analysis of data.

Reading First: a grant program to provide money for the teaching of reading in American schools. Grants were awarded only to schools that adopted highly structured (scripted) reading materials from a few publishers that the administration favors as being "scientific."

Socially constructed: a seminal term in interpretivism, which holds that all knowledge is socially constructed. That is, the world consists not of a single independent reality, but instead of multiple realities constructed by people whose perceptions vary with their backgrounds.

Teacher inquiry/Teacher research: Catch-all, ill-defined terms used to refer to multiple models of educational action research; either term's meaning in a specific context depends upon the purposes and processes of the model.

Trustworthiness: a quality standard for interpretive action research which refers to how credible an audience may find a particular study, based on such factors as whether the amount and type of data collected seem appropriate.

Variable: one factor that appears to influence another, so that a change in one correlates with a change in the other. For example, an educational researcher might study whether an increase in nightly homework correlates with higher standardized test scores.

NOTE

1. Some writers note a third category, called *technical,* in which practitioners try out recommendations from expert researchers. Most theorists argue, however, that such research does not qualify as action research because it aligns with the positivist paradigm and it places the practitioner in a position subordinate to the expert researcher.

CHAPTER THREE

Developing a Research Plan and Identifying a Research Question

Developing a Research Plan

As this text moves from general information to an outline of the action research process, a caution from Noffke (1997) is appropriate:

> Defining action research in terms of a particular process or series of steps may help to identify it as a research technique, but in so doing one also clouds the issues of the purposes to which it is advanced: the political agendas, both overt and embedded in the constructions of the professional and personal. (333)

Readers are urged, as they begin exploring the *how* aspect of action research, to keep in mind that more important is the *why*. Although examples in the following material often focus on pedagogical issues, these were selected only for clarity and are not intended to endorse some models of action research over others. Readers will need to remember that the basic information on process offered here can be adjusted to a wide variety of goals, commitments and contexts.

A Perspective on Research Process

Despite significant variation in action research models, each involves the same core activities. Though often described as having three phases (Stringer, 2004; Hendricks, 2006; Schmuck, 2006), any action research project requires several practical steps:

- Developing a question
- Formulating a research plan
- Systematically collecting data
- Analyzing the data
- Developing and implementing an action plan
- Recording the project in writing

Many models additionally suggest sharing the study with others.

This neat step-by-step progression is not, however, as tidy as it looks on paper.

Although the components of the process appear **linear**, action research is actually often **recursive** in practice. That is, although it is often explained as a process consisting of chronological steps (first develop a question, then formulate a research plan, and so on), researchers commonly move back and forth among various activities, for the simple reason that later work often produces ideas for useful changes to original plans. For example, a teacher researcher might plan to analyze one marking period of a student's writing. However, after collecting that data and beginning analysis, the teacher might sense a pattern but want more data to substantiate it. At that point, he might interrupt analyzing to collect more data, modifying the original plan by adding work from a second marking period. Similarly, a group of parents and educators might begin a study to assess effectiveness of a charter school; after beginning data collection, they might realize that they had not planned to obtain information from students about their experiences. At that point, the researchers might add a new question about student perceptions, develop an additional strategy for data collection, and perhaps invite student representatives to join the initial group and participate in data analysis and action planning. As a study progresses and researchers develop deeper understanding, it is not unusual for them to change their original plans. Therefore, while it's important to become familiar with various steps of the process, it's equally

Linear

proceeding from one point to another in a straight line.

Recursive

involving repetition; in educational research, used to describe a process in which researchers move back and forth among various phases of the research—from data analysis to additional data collection, for example.

important to understand that the process is a flexible tool for the researcher's purposes—not a rigid and restrictive regimen.

Basics of the Research Plan

Research plan/research brief

a plan detailing the several steps of an action research project; typically, it includes at a minimum the study's purpose, question/s, methods, and time line.

Any purposeful journey has a planned route to a specific destination. In action research, a **research plan** (or **research brief**) identifies a destination and maps the route the researcher will follow to arrive there. The research destination is the answer to a particular question (for example, What is causing this problem?), and the plan offers the researcher/driver directions on how to get there. Just as drivers may encounter unexpected detours, action researchers may be surprised by unexpected events as the process unfolds and find themselves adjusting their plans en route. Still, without a beginning plan, any study might easily become an aimless ramble. The act of planning helps minimize time spent backtracking—or facing dead ends.

Generally, developing a research plan involves thinking through the answers to a set of questions that then serve as a set of instructions for the researcher to follow. Research plans detail not only *what* needs to be done but also *when* and *how* each step will be accomplished. They also include a statement of purpose, or a summary of what the researcher hopes the work will accomplish. The purpose statement helps keep the project focused and provides a touchstone useful when the researcher must choose among questions and methods.

A list developed by Hubbard and Power (1999) offers an accessible and useful overview of elements common to research plans:

Research purpose:	Why do I want to study this?
Research question:	What do I want to study? What subquestions do I have?
Data collection:	How will I collect data?
Data analysis:	How will I analyze my data?
Time line:	When will I complete the different phases of my study?
Support:	Who will help me sustain this project?
Permissions:	What permissions do I need to collect? Are there ethical issues to consider? (pp. 47–48)

While this outline may suggest that a research plan document will resemble a sort of outline, in fact format is irrelevant. The purpose of the plan is to provide support for the researcher, and so any format the researcher finds useful is fine. A plan could very well consist of a list of answers to those questions—or it might look more like a memo, or an essay, with a paragraph on each topic and/ or headings appearing here and there. Format will vary with researcher, which is fine. What is important is not how the final product looks, but how well it has been thought out.

Time lines

A schedule for the research project is critical. It can be intensely frustrating to realize that an opportunity to collect data appeared...yesterday. It is equally futile to collect data and then let it sit in a file drawer untouched for months. Practitioners are all busy people who most often carve research time from an already overfull schedule; self-imposed deadlines help prevent the research project from slipping onto some eternally simmering back burner. Momentum matters, and a timeline can serve as a constant reminder of time passing and work waiting.

Many researchers find it helpful to plan backward—to start with a targeted end date and then allocate the amount of time available for the work. If, for example, summer would provide good time for the researcher to complete data analysis and formulate findings, then the deadline for data collection would logically be the end of the school year. Once the end date for collection is set, a starting date can be determined, depending upon the amount of data wanted and the difficulty of obtaining it. As will be discussed momentarily, collection of some data may require obtaining permissions first. Therefore, the starting day of data collection would also serve as the deadline for securing permissions. And so on.

While setting a time line appears such an obvious and easy task that novices might be tempted to skip it, time is a precious commodity that must be spent with great care. Otherwise, a project is likely to be weakened by some of its necessary components being too rushed. Planning— and meeting—deadlines for various phases of the work improves project quality *and* saves the researcher/s stress. If a question is too big for the time available, it can be

modified before the project starts rather than desperately hacked down to size as research progresses.

Support

While not all research plans consider sources of support, it can be worth the researcher's time to think through which colleagues, or others, might be able to provide insights on the work as it moves forward. This is especially true for individual researchers, who can benefit from discussing their thinking with others who understand their situations and purposes—a friend in another district, teachers in the same school, a mentor, another researcher, perhaps a research group. The question to ask is "Who can help me think critically about this project as it moves from phase to phase?" Discussions with such colleagues can help determine if a plan is feasible and complete, if interpretation of data seems reasonable or questionable, and if the action suggestions appear logical next steps.

Another way to think about the support question is to ask "Whose support will make it more likely that this project will be successful during and after implementation?" For example, some administrators might not initially be pleased to hear that someone in the school plans to analyze the tracking system to determine if its results may be discriminatory. Since no one wants to be associated with discriminatory practices—and because changing something as significant as tracking would require widespread support—the researcher might plan initial meetings with a variety of stakeholders to assure them that the intent is to identify *unintentional* bias. The point could be strengthened if the researcher did a preliminary **literature review** to identify other studies indicating that despite authorities' best intentions, tracking systems intended to be neutral can nevertheless produce discriminatory results. Sharing such reports from others' experiences can be very helpful in eliciting cooperation from local authorities. Especially when an issue may be a sensitive one for other stakeholders, such groundwork can be enormously helpful to the eventual success and impact of a project—but it takes advance planning and time.

In thinking through the research plan, then, researchers should consider who can be a good springboard for ideas and a constructive critic, and whose "buy-in" is necessary for the work to accomplish its intended objec-

Literature review

written summary of published material related to a research topic; researchers often conduct literature reviews for ideas on study design and/or to make connections between their new study and others that have come before.

tives. Depending on the objective of a particular study, how to secure that buy-in may be a significant strategic question.

Permissions and ethics

In some cases, support is not simply desirable and helpful, as noted above, but *essential*. Formal permission may be necessary to access particular kinds of data. For example, researchers interested in identifying unacknowledged health issues among students would need access to student health records, which are, by law, confidential. Before beginning the study, researchers would need to determine whether such access would be legal; if so, whether district authorities would be willing to grant it; and if they were, how the privacy of individual students would be protected. Legality, confidentiality, and sensitivity about negative information can all pose significant obstacles in accessing potential data, and researchers must be sure to confirm very early in their efforts that they will be able to get the data they need.

Even when the data seem readily accessible—as when a teacher plans to use student work—ethical concerns may dictate the need for formal permission. All research traditions have ethical guidelines to protect research participants; in action research specifically, two primary ethical concerns are participants' privacy/confidentiality and the researcher's potential abuse of power. For example, students' right to privacy can be violated when researchers share such information as student essays or comments publicly, especially if individual students can be easily identified. Abuse of power is also a concern when the researcher has power over the participants (as teachers do over students); participants should never be coerced into contributing data for a study. Thus, research projects often involve securing formal agreement from participants to provide information and/or allow information to be shared in some way.

However: because action research projects and purposes are so variable, guidelines for when such formal permission is necessary in AR projects are somewhat flexible (or, unclear may be a more accurate term, since there is significant disagreement on the issue). Generally, whether participants' permission is needed for a study depends upon how public the process and results will be. A teacher

working alone, only in his classroom, studying only normal daily activities, and planning to use the results only to inform his own practice, would not need any special permission for a project. In this case, the action research process would simply be a formal version of the kind of analytical thinking all teachers do routinely; no student can be threatened by it because the teacher will not share any of the data or thinking with anyone else.

If, on the other hand, the researcher were planning to share information in any way—by presenting results of the project to some group, or writing for publication, for example—the situation changes. In such cases, permission would need to be formally obtained from legal guardians for children under age 18, and from students themselves if they are 18 or older. To address confidentiality concerns, researchers often guarantee participants anonymity; they may promise to omit names, to use pseudonyms, or to employ such generic phrases as "Some students felt that...." Researchers must remember that sharing information involves publicly projecting some image of the participants, whose rights and sensitivities are as important as the researcher's goals.[1]

Ethical guidelines for educational research in general have been detailed by the American Educational Research Association (AERA) and many other professional organizations, and Zeni (1998) has published an article on practitioner research that outlines a useful "alternative guide with questions suited to action research" (abstract) (see Resources).

Informed consent form
used to secure and document the willingness of persons to participate in a research study. The form describes the purpose and methods of research and such other topics as how confidentiality will be ensured.

When formal permission is necessary, it is documented with **informed consent forms**. These are documents that participants or their legal guardians sign to indicate that they agree to participate in the project. Typically, such forms outline why the study is being conducted, what methods will be used, how confidentiality will be assured, and how a participant who changes her mind may withdraw. Consent forms summarize such information so that when the appropriate person signs, there is a formal record of the agreement and its terms. Samples and guidelines for informed consent forms are readily available online from university websites and in many textbooks on action research (for example, Hubbard & Power, 1999; Stringer, 2004; Hendricks, 2006). Figure 3, however, provides a generic sample.

FIGURE 3: SAMPLE INFORMED CONSENT FORM

Study of Student Writing: Permission Request

Dear Parent/Guardian,

 I am planning to study sentence structure typical of our ninth grade students. I plan to base this study on that writing students do during our regular class work. My purpose is to identify which sentence structures students typically use correctly, which incorrectly, and which don't appear at all. The information gained from the study will be used by the ninth grade English team to adjust our curriculum for next year. While I may report on this study in a conference presentation or an article, I will protect student anonymity in any public reports of this work. Should I share specific examples of student writing, I will be sure there is no way to link any one example to a specific student or class.

   By signing this form, you indicate that you have given permission for me to use the written work of your child in this study and perhaps to quote from it, protecting your child's anonymity, in public reports of the work. Should you change your mind, you need only provide me with written instructions to exclude your child's work.

Signature:

Date:

A word on literature review

As indicated above, the literature review is a summary of what has already been written on the topic under study. Interpretivists use literature reviews as a practical means of saving time and/or advancing thinking by learning what others have already said and done in an area. While not all AR models call for a literature review, many do. Some incorporate it as an early component of the research plan, for an obvious and sensible reason: time a practitioner might spend "reinventing the wheel" would likely be better spent trying out a wheel someone else already designed. If a teacher is struggling with a particular pedagogical issue, it's likely others have already dealt with the same issue and developed useful strategies. It can make good sense to save time by looking through published material for ideas, and listing a few key documents in the research plan can provide a good start for the process. The reference section of particularly relevant documents can point the way to still other useful materials.

Other models suggest completing a literature review during or after data analysis to help make sense of new

information the study provided. Have others reported seeing the same thing? Have they interpreted similar data the same way? For example, a teacher whose study had documented test-related stress and illness among students might wonder whether other teachers had reported the same. If she explored the existing literature, she would find that they had, and that what at first seemed a local issue is actually part of a national problem needing attention on multiple levels—local, state and national. In addition, the literature review might offer information on strategies others had used successfully, or even suggestions for state and national groups that she might consider joining.

Moreover, if practitioners are to build a new knowledge base, it is important for them to help tie numerous individual studies together into a coherent whole. From this perspective, it is extremely valuable for researchers to read what others have reported and to place their own findings into a larger context when they report on them. A significant knowledge base can grow only through such connections.

In short, even though not all models explicitly suggest one, a literature review is informative and useful. In formulating a research plan, researchers should consider the possibility of including one. Many resources are available electronically, and sophisticated search engines and databases have made identifying and locating them much easier. Libraries, especially university libraries, offer extensive access to multiple databases which provide full text copies of many documents, including journal articles that at one time were available only in print. Help with a literature review is often available from someone facilitating an action research process and from university or other librarians.

While these components are staples of research plans, they are neither exhaustive nor prescriptive. Researchers can add any other information that might seem useful: anticipated difficulties, the target audience for an eventual report, warning reminders to themselves ("Be careful not to get sidetracked while doing the library research!")... anything likely to keep the project focused and moving forward. The more detailed a research plan is, the more useful it can be to the researcher.

Figure 4 provides an illustration of what a typical research plan might look like based on the suggestions in this chapter.

FIGURE 4: SAMPLE RESEARCH PLAN

Plan for Sentence Structure Study

Purpose: To identify instructional opportunities for improving the correctness and maturity of ninth graders' typical sentence structure. (Tenth grade teachers have complained that overall, students rely heavily on simple and coordinate constructions. Students complain they have a hard time getting sentences to say what they mean/intend.)

Research Question: What sentence structures are typical of ninth grade students' writing? To what extent are they using those structures correctly?

Sub-Questions: For each sentence type: (simple, compound, complex, compound-complex), do students:
- Use the structure in their writing?
- If so, how often?
- If so, how often correctly, how often not?
- If so, how often does structure seem to match emphasis (simple sentences for maximum emphasis, less important ideas in subordinate clauses, etc.)

Data Collection: I will copy: 1) my ninth grade students' responses to the first marking period's two essay assignments, and 2) two samples of in-class writing assignments.

Data Analysis: I will color code each sentence to indicate its structure and assign a minus sign (–) to any sentence containing a structural error. I will use these codings to determine how often and how correctly students use various structures. Matching intended emphasis to structure will be more complicated; I will need to design some form that will allow a few independent raters to identify cases of obviously appropriate and inappropriate match-ups of form with emphasis.

Time Line: Data collection: end of first marking period

Data analysis: initial analysis to be completed during fall break; independent ratings of correlation between structure and meaning by January 5

Written report: to be shared with ninth grade team one week before March in-service day to allow for discussion there.

Support: Members of the team, or English teachers from other grade levels, will be needed to do independent analyses of structure/intent. I should also ask them to help me design the form.

Permissions: needed from parents and/or guardians

Identifying a Research Question

To return to a metaphor invoked above: research can be conceptualized as a way to reach some destination—

that destination being the answer to a research question. Everything in the research process flows from the research question, just as every set of driving directions depends upon the destination. Before deciding to take a north/south or east/west interstate highway, the driver has to consider where he intends to arrive.

Obviously, choosing the wrong question, or wording a question inappropriately, can derail a project before it's even begun. Therefore, this section focuses on the critical issues of identifying and wording useful research questions.

Identifying a Research Interest

Experience

Educators are people in the habit of thinking and wondering. They fret about something that went wrong, or they consider how something might be better, or they try to puzzle out an explanation for a phenomenon they don't understand, or they wonder what would happen if they tried that new technique they read about the other day. Because they tend to be naturally curious people genuinely interested in their students, practitioners rarely have difficulty identifying a general interest area for a research project. Poor student grades or behavior or standardized test scores, inadequate classroom supplies or student support services, pervasive student health problems, discriminatory language and practices in the school, a tracking system that reflects socioeconomic status more than ability: many schools have not only such problems but also stakeholders interested in addressing them. Or, rather than focusing a problem, a researcher can take a closer look at elements of school routine that have long gone unquestioned: "This has always been our hiring process—but how does it compare to other districts' practices?" "We've assumed we can't afford not to comply with No Child Left Behind—but what exactly would the costs of non-compliance be?" Or, a researcher might simply seek a better understanding of some relevant topic, asking such questions as: "What elements of the curriculum do students find most and least useful?" "How might incorporating a community service requirement affect students and the community?"

All of which is to say that a researcher's questions come from a researcher's experience: from what happened

yesterday or today, from what might or could happen tomorrow, from the nagging worry that pops up every morning in the shower, or the unexpected tears of a distraught student, or the surprised grin of the tough guy who earned an A on a paper. Hubbard and Power (1999) suggest that questions come from "tensions" and "gaps" in the researcher's experience; Dana & Yendol Silva (2003) cite Sherman's term (1997) "felt difficulties." In short, any concern or interest that grows out of practice can provide the seed of an action research project.

It's far more common for a researcher to have difficulty choosing among possibilities than to have difficulty identifying *an* interest. Still: newcomers to the process sometimes feel lost when they begin considering a research topic. Most often, that is because they are haunted by images of positivist research and tend to feel that their interests aren't big enough or important enough: "Why is Chris so angelic some days, so disruptive others?" "Why do those three students seem to hate what all other students seem to love?" While these may seem small and routine questions to some teachers, either could prompt a useful action research study, since each seeks information that could help the researcher improve teaching and learning. Because better understanding leads to better practice, few of a practitioner's real questions aren't worth the time and trouble necessary to study them—and those few are fairly easily identified and avoided. Generally, they are questions that the researcher can already answer, and questions that have yes/no answers (Hubbard and Power, 1999).

Since action research is intended to provide the researcher with useful information, there's no point in conducting a study to demonstrate what she already knows. Yes/no questions are similarly unhelpful because they yield minimal information. Often, for example, they hide the fact that a study is intended to support an opinion a researcher already holds—another version of asking a question when the answer is already known. A teacher secretly proud of giving difficult reading quizzes might ask "Are my reading quizzes challenging for students?" simply to confirm his reputation. While such a study might give the teacher some satisfaction in seeing that opinion confirmed, it offers no information useful in improving anything. Of course, there's always the chance that the researcher would be surprised to get information contrary to his beliefs, in which

case the study might be valuable—but not if the question asked required only a yes/no answer.

Suppose, for example, that this researcher believed the quizzes were easy but students said no, they aren't. What would that "no" mean? There are multiple possibilities, each having drastically different implications for practice. It might mean that students believe the instructor consciously makes quizzes impossible by basing them on unimportant details or by using tricky questions in order to keep grades low, stroking his own ego with a reputation for toughness. In stark contrast, it might mean that students believe that the quizzes are easy only when they take time to do assigned reading carefully and thoughtfully; in this case, students saying the quizzes are not easy would be a good thing since it reflects a positive impact on both student motivation and student-teacher relationships. Of course, different students in a single class could conceivably hold each of these views—and perhaps others as well. The most important information in a study like this one would not be *that* students held a particular opinion, but *why*. In this case, for example, rather than asking the yes/no question "Are my quizzes challenging?" the researcher might more usefully ask "How do my students perceive my reading quizzes? Why?" A great deal more useful information is likely to come out of such open-ended questions.

Typical Areas of Educational Action Research

While any area of experience can prompt a good action research study, analyses of completed studies indicate that educators typically probe several specific areas (Dana & Yendol-Silva, 2003; Holly et al., 2005, for example). There is a growing body of work in each area that can provide researchers with ideas for research topics and designs and that allows them to compare their findings with others.

An individual child or group of children. Because educators have an intrinsic interest in children, action researchers often focus on a particular child or group of children. All teachers have struggled with how to better meet the needs of a particular student: one who is failing, or painfully shy, or dangerously bored, or openly hostile, or consistently sorrowful. Each child is unique and has unique needs, so that the educator's attention often focuses on this child or that, whichever seems most in need of attention at a particular time. Sometimes that attention turns to groups of stu-

dents who share similar characteristics (being in the same socioeconomic group, clique or track) or who face similar challenges (mastering English as a second language, dealing with physical limitations). These studies essentially ask "How can I/we make the school experience more productive and enjoyable for this child/these children?"

The curriculum. Although many people perceive curriculum as something simple and obvious (history: Columbus), it involves much more than presenting information on given topics. The teacher instructed to cover the "discovery" of America would, of course, include in the unit the information that U.S. textbooks generally credit Columbus with the discovery in 1492.[2] However, other large choices loom. Possible related topics include such widely varied areas as: the economic motives that drove exploration; the hardships endured in the long journey across the Atlantic; that several tribes and cultures were on the continent for centuries before Columbus arrived—and that they were, perhaps, descendants of earlier Asian explorers; that, in any case, many historians believe that Chinese and Viking explorers predated Columbus; or, the devastating impact of European diseases, guns and "civilization" on the native peoples. Possible objectives are equally varied, including such alternatives as students learning that: Columbus was a great explorer worthy of admiration; great accomplishments often involve great personal risk and sacrifice; the same events look different to different people; some of today's social problems can be traced through centuries of historical events; readers should seek out various sources of information on a topic and reach their own conclusions.

Few curriculum guides explore such alternatives, and an action research project can provide practitioners with the focus and structure to think them through. Alternatively stated, action research projects can help educators translate general curricular imperatives to coherent classroom units. Similarly, administrators and policymakers might use action research to learn how educators translate the exhortation to "Use more technology in teaching and learning" into practice, or to explore whether a particular sex education curriculum is having the intended effect—or if stakeholders are even familiar with the intended effect. Questions in this category often take the general form of "What should this curriculum include and accomplish in

the classroom?" and "What effects does this curriculum have on teaching and learning?"

Teaching strategies. Deciding what to teach is one thing; deciding how to teach it is another. Because every teacher daily confronts the question of how best to teach something, education action research projects frequently focus on pedagogy. For example, an elementary teacher might be using weekly word lists and tests to teach vocabulary but be dissatisfied with the results: students pass the tests but don't use the new words when speaking or writing. The teacher might study the effects of an additional activity ("What happens when I make a habit of using vocabulary words in my everyday speech and encourage students to do the same?"), or of an alternative strategy ("What happens when I allow students to create individual vocabulary lists based on their reading and experience?").

Generally, teachers might study what happens when they try a new method, or which methods seem best suited to which topics and/or students, or what conditions are necessary for a method to be effective. A study of pedagogy can uncover both intended and unintended consequences—as when an emphasis on test scores raises grades but increases cheating as well. Or, it can help teachers understand how best to vary assessment methods so that the students who excel on essays and those who do best on objective, multiple choice exams will both have an opportunity to shine. Or, it can help teachers probe what conditions are necessary for certain teaching strategies to be effective ("How much and what kind of structure do my students need to complete assignments successfully in small groups?"). Pedagogical questions often ask "What happens when I _____?" or "What is the most effective way to help students learn _____?" or "What might be the preconditions for this teaching method to be effective in my class?"

Administrators and policy makers might also look at pedagogy, especially in a time when particular methodologies are being widely promoted. A typical contemporary action research project at this level might, for example, ask something like "What impact is our mandated reading program having on test scores, student perceptions of reading, and teacher satisfaction?" Or, "How well do our teaching strategies as a school community align with our

goal of educating students to become independent thinkers and creative problem solvers?"

Previously unexamined beliefs. Although we are often unaware of our assumptions, they guide many of our actions. Teachers may assume, for example, either that parents care very much about their children's education—and so communicate with them frequently—or that parents don't care at all—and so ignore them, or deplore them. Unfortunately, it's all too easy to adopt an unfounded, or only partially valid, assumption. Perhaps some parents don't care—but many do; perhaps all of them care—but don't have the background to help their children with schoolwork, or are working two jobs to keep food on the table, or have had miserable school experiences themselves that make them reluctant to approach a school or teacher. Or: perhaps a child isn't living with parents at all.

The only way to be sure any given assumption is valid is to test it, as action researchers often do. In this case, for example, a study might explore the question "How do the caregivers in our students' lives perceive education? What are the sources of those perceptions?" As in every other area, studies might also ask more ambitious questions. For example, it is widely assumed that business should have a voice in shaping schools, especially in terms of curriculum. A representative school community group might choose to ask "What role—if any—do we believe the business community should have in influencing our policy and curriculum? What are the justifications for that stance, and are they credible?"

Such studies open up the possibility that responses will make the rationale for good policies explicit while confirming assumptions—or that they will produce an entirely new range of ideas. Questions about assumptions generally ask "How do others see this?" or "Why is this the case?"

Alignment of personal and professional identity. Asked what they believe in as people, few educators would have trouble answering: integrity, or democracy, or independence, or kindness, or respect, or any of an endless list of values. Professing a value is easy, but living a value, especially by incorporating it into professional practice, can be difficult indeed. For example, teachers often insist that it's important for students to learn responsibility by meeting deadlines—but fail repeatedly to return graded papers on

a promised date; they insist that students be respectful in their speech—but are often sarcastic themselves; they praise democracy—but run autocratic classrooms; they encourage creativity—but accept work only within a narrow range of possibilities. Everyone, including students, is quick to note, and typically resent, the hypocrisy of such discrepancies between word and deed.

Many practitioners use action research to more consciously align their professed personal values with their professional identity. Examples might include studies that ask "Which practices in my classroom are democratic and which are not?" or "How do I model—or undermine—the value of honesty in my classroom?" or "How do I model for my students the importance of standing up for an unpopular idea?" Similarly, administrators might ask "In what ways do our policies promote a sense of professionalism among teachers? In what ways do they undermine it and signal that teachers can't be trusted?" or "In what ways do we signal to students that we believe each of them can learn and be successful? In what ways do we suggest otherwise?" Studies in this area generally ask "What do we do that models this professed value, and what do we do that undermines it?"

Social justice. Many educators have adopted the critical perspective that assigns everyone, and especially educators, responsibility for working toward a more just and equitable world. Action research studies in this case often seek either to uncover possible inequities or to work toward strategies to address demonstrably inequitable situations. It is not uncommon, for example, to hear educators speak disrespectfully of particular students—of those who may come to school in unclean clothes, or those whose dress might be considered provocative or outrageous. It is also not uncommon for such students to be tracked into the lowest classes, where they may receive disrespectful treatment. Studies in such cases might ask questions like: "What is the correlation between students' socioeconomic status and the tracks they are placed in?" "Which students have experienced disrespectful treatment by school personnel? What characteristics do they share?" "How can we develop a school climate in which everyone receives equally respectful treatment?"

Administrators and policymakers might similarly ask "How has this policy affected various groups of students?"

to determine whether a particular policy has had inequitable impact. For example, a research group in one district might ask "How has No Child Left Behind affected our students as compared to its impact on students in our neighboring, more affluent district?" Or, it might ask "How have our disciplinary policies been applied to students from different socioeconomic backgrounds?" Questions in this area generally ask "What are the experiences of [this particular group of students]? If and where inequities appear, how might they be remedied?"

Because critical theory stresses giving voice to those whose voices are rarely heard (students on the lowest level of the school's hierarchy; parents who do not speak English, for example), studies in this area are often ambitious and conducted by research groups that include a wide variety of community representatives—educators, parents/caregivers, local government officials, social workers, and so on. Studies pursuing social justice often fit within the participatory action research (PAR) paradigm. In general, they ask "What do various stakeholders in this community see as a problem? What are their suggestions for making improvements?" or "What are the causes of this problematic situation? How can we work together to improve it?"

Context. Every school is affected by surrounding circles of community, state, federal and other national influences. Schools reflect their community members—who may look and think very differently than the teachers in them. (While some half of all students are neither White nor middle class, teachers are overwhelmingly both.) States may change educational policies every few years; federal initiatives like the Civil Rights laws and No Child Left Behind can cause tremendous upheaval; conflicts between such forces as religion and government can produce national movements like that seeking to prevent science teachers from discussing evolution.

Therefore, it is not unusual for understanding of a local issue to require an understanding of the larger context influencing events. On a modest, practical level, teachers might ask something like "Given that I know most of my students have working parents and limited resources, what are reasonable requirements for independent projects that involve buying materials and adult supervision?" Or, many types of larger questions are possible: "What values are typical among residents of this community? How can our school community reflect and honor those values?" "How can we adapt our practice to this new state requirement without undermining already successful elements of our practice?" "What strategies can we use to minimize the potential negative impact of No Child Left Behind?" "How can we best address parental concerns about the teaching of evolution?"

In essence, studies of context ask "What elements of our environment need to be accommodated in our practice? What are the best strategies for that accommodation?"

Content? Some texts include the possibility of action research projects focusing on subject matter content—not to make curricular choices, as discussed above, but to remedy a gap in a teacher's preparation or to help a teacher prepare for an new, emergency assignment. While it is certainly the case that such preparation involves research, and the teacher will act as a result of it, it is questionable whether this type of research truly constitutes action research as most commonly conceptualized, as work unique in being centered in specific local conditions. Anyone anywhere might choose to read about any topic—work that seems much more like traditional library research than action research.

Still, when action research is conceptualized primarily as professional development in the interest of improving practice, then the argument can be made for action research projects that focus on expanding the practitioner's knowledge of academic content. A question in this area would ask "What do I need to know about this topic in order to competently (or better) teach it?"

Limiting Questions

Once committed to a general area of study, the researcher has to wrestle with the task of appropriately clarifying and limiting a specific question. Wording matters, because the exact wording of a question drives every other element of a study. Two questions arising from the same concern (too many students failing exams, for example) can produce two very different studies. For example, "How can I encourage students to study harder for exams?" leads in a very different direction than "Why do students fail so many of my exams?" In addition, questions can be more or less focused, more or less manageable. The question "What do parents/caregivers think of our school and teachers?" is too broad to be useful. Does the researcher want to

know if they are happy with the food in the cafeteria, the hours of classes, the amount of homework, the curriculum, the bus drivers and routes, the credentials of the teachers, the amount of respect staff show students, the quality of the athletic program, the cleanliness of the bathrooms, the availability of teachers, the academic preparation of teachers, school-to-home communications, the safety of the building... *what?* Overly broad questions produce a hodge-podge of information, so that making sense of the data can be difficult or impossible. Well-focused questions are essential to good projects.

Generally, it takes researchers considerable time and thought to clearly identify what they actually want to know. For example, after reflection, a researcher who started with a general question about what parents/caregivers think might decide that her real interest is whether they are satisfied with student learning—a much narrower territory. Or, perhaps a school research group became interested in how the school is perceived because group members consider parents/caregivers difficult to work with. Wondering whether some negative perceptions were circulating in the community, the research group might usefully limit the overly broad question above to something like "What positive and negative impressions do parents/caregivers generally seem to have of their child/children's experience in our school? What are the sources of these impressions?" This version limits the research to determining how a particular group perceives students' experiences and uncovering links between those perceptions and what generated them.

Heuristic
a strategy to advance learning or problem-solving.

Stringer (2004) offers a useful **heuristic** for moving from a general interest or concern to a specific research question. His advice is to:

- Define the issue/event/curiosity that prompts the study (often a description of the problem)
- Explain what problem/concern the issue presents
- Reword the problem/concern into the form of a question
- Describe what the researcher hopes will happen as a result of the study

Applied to one of the examples from the above, the process might produce work like the following:

- The issue: Given what I know about Pat's experience, I am worried that some of our students might be disciplined more harshly than others for the same offenses.
- The problem: Such treatment would be inequitable, and since students are quick to recognize unfairness, those treated more harshly are likely to become resentful toward school authorities and hostile toward the school.
- The question: How have our disciplinary policies been applied to different groups of students? If and where inequities appear, how might they be remedied and avoided in the future?
- The objective: To monitor and promote equitable treatment of different groups of students.

While this linear presentation looks fairly simple and straightforward, researchers can expect to spend some time working through the thinking process to clarify exactly what they want to accomplish and why. Stringer's method offers a useful path through that frequently muddy terrain.

Two more useful bits of advice come from Hubbard and Power (1999), who additionally suggest making an effort to edit jargon and value-laden words out of research questions. Jargon is not helpful because it can obscure meaning. For example, the question "What is the effect of our scripted reading program on teaching and learning?" will make no sense to anyone unfamiliar with the term "scripted," or may be interpreted differently by different readers/researchers. This question might be more clearly worded as "What effect do materials that tell teachers what to say and do in every lesson have on teaching and learning?" Eliminating jargon promotes clarity and avoids value-laden bias. The specific wording of a question can shift its focus and slant what the research will find. For example, the question "How does the new reading program constrict teachers' classroom performance?" has already made a negative value judgment about the program, evident in the verb *constrict;* by focusing on negative limitations, the question excludes the possibility of getting evidence of other possible effects. A better question for genuine understanding of the issue would be the more neutral "How do teachers say the new reading program has affected their classroom performance?"

Sub-Questions

Sub-questions
smaller questions that must be answered in the course of answering a larger question.

Any substantive research question has **sub-questions** that must be articulated and answered as part of the study. Before comparing treatment of student groups, for example, it would be necessary to first identify *which* groups to compare. There are, after all, various ways to describe students, each highlighting different characteristics. School staff might casually refer to students by socio-economic status ("His parents have more money than they can spend."); by academic track ("He's college prep."); by appearance ("Soon he'll be sitting on that pony tail."); by academic performance ("He's an A student."). Thus, for the question "How have our disciplinary problems been applied to different groups of students?" a necessary sub-question would be "Which categories/groups do school personnel seem to reference most often when referring to students?" The answer to that question would allow researchers to make an informed decision about which groups might be most productively compared for their larger purposes.

Or, for the more ambitious question "What would non-compliance with NCLB cost our district?" an inherent sub-question would be "What are the various cost areas associated with NCLB?" Of course, money is involved, but an answer to the sub-question about all relevant areas would include in addition stress for students and teachers, impact on curriculum and school morale, increases in the dropout rate, and so on. An answer to the first sub-question ("What *are* the various kinds of costs?") would provide direction for the multiple areas to be examined.

Scope
in research literature, the limits of the work; what will be included or excluded.

Thinking through sub-questions can also help researchers limit the general **scope** of a study. Researchers working to tease out sub-questions may realize that they lack critical resources—time or access to information—to answer a particular sub-question, indicating a need to rework the major question. In the above, for example, researchers might realize that determining the financial cost of administering NCLB's high-stakes testing is beyond their expertise and capacity, since experts argue strenuously about how such cost should be calculated and, in any event, the district has no recordkeeping system that would allow for disaggregating NCLB costs. Thus, they might reframe their original question as "What non-financial

costs is the district experiencing in its efforts to comply with NCLB?"

On the whole, identifying the question/s for a study is a complex process that may well require more time and thought than novices may anticipate. However: the process should never be rushed since the success and usefulness of the study depend on the researcher accurately identifying the research destination.

GLOSSARY

Heuristic: a strategy to advance learning or problem-solving.

Informed consent form: used to secure and document the willingness of persons to participate in a research study. The form describes the purpose and methods of research and such other topics as how confidentiality will be ensured.

Linear: proceeding from one point to another in a straight line.

Literature review: written summary of published material related to a research topic; researchers often conduct literature reviews for ideas on study design and/or to make connections between their new study and others that have come before.

Recursive: involving repetition; in educational research, used to describe a process in which researchers move back and forth among various phases of the research—from data analysis to additional data collection, for example.

Research plan/research brief: a plan detailing the several steps of an action research project; typically, it includes at a minimum the study's purpose, question/s, methods, and time line.

Scope: in research literature, the limits of the work; what will be included or excluded.

Sub-questions: smaller questions that must be answered in the course of answering a larger question.

NOTE

1. An interesting and readable article that makes obvious how quickly ethical issues can surface in and complicate action research is Sharon K. Miller's 2001 article, "Lessons from Tony: Betrayal and Trust in Teacher Research." Available from http://www.nwp.org/cs/public/print/resource/149.

2. For an interesting example of how some classroom teachers worked through a curriculum on this particular topic, see Dana & Yendol-Silva (2003), p. 24–26.

CHAPTER FOUR

Collecting and Analyzing Data

Collecting Data

Quality and Quantity

To determine reliable answers to research questions, researchers must make careful decisions about what kind, and how much, data to collect. Like other elements of research design, the task may appear deceptively easy. For example, researchers are often inclined to collect grades as evidence of almost anything: ability, interest, work ethic, respect for education... among many others. Grades do indicate something—but *what* they indicate is often debatable so that they are useful in far fewer instances than one might think.

Suppose, for example, that researchers wanted to know "To what extent are students engaged in these classes?" An initial impulse might be to collect grades as indicators, on the assumption that high engagement produces good grades, weak engagement, poor grades. However, as anyone who has ever been a student knows, the assumed relationship between grades and engagement is hardly reliable. Students might experience a class as irrelevant and boring but earn an A simply because the work is both minimal

and easy. Or in contrast, students might find themselves mesmerized by course content and be thoroughly engaged, and yet earn only Cs because the work is so challenging. It can be difficult to assign meaning to data confidently under the best conditions; collecting ambiguous data only makes the task harder and, potentially, the study less credible. Better data in this case, for example, might come from an anonymous survey of students directly asking them about their experiences in and perception of the courses. While some question may remain as to how reliable and thorough the students' responses were, the researcher can be far more confident that they bear directly on the research question.

Another way that researchers minimize ambiguity in their findings is by using **triangulation**. That is, they frequently collect multiple types of data—minimally three—to increase confidence in their findings. To explore the impact of tracking on students, for example, researchers might: examine statistical records and correlate neighborhoods with placements (since neighborhoods are generally indicative of socioeconomic status); interview guidance counselors about their interactions with students and administrators relevant to student placement in particular tracks; and, survey students about their experiences with placement and instruction in their tracks. If the same information appears in all three sources, then its credibility is stronger than if the study relied on only one type of data.

It is also important to have sufficient data collected over an appropriate length of time. For example, it would be inappropriate to base judgments about a student on a single day of observations in a single class. Anyone, a student or anyone else, can perform very differently on one day than on another, for such varied reasons as health and sleep issues, moods, worries, time to prepare, and so on. Data from a single observation can therefore record typical behavior—or atypical behavior. Credible inferences would require far more information, over a longer period of time. Time span can, in fact, be a crucial factor. For example, many studies use surveys or exams immediately after instruction to determine whether a particular teaching strategy was effective; however, more rigorous studies ask not how well students recall material immediately after instruction, but also a week, a month, or several months

Triangulation
to collect three different types of data relevant to the same question in order to increase the likelihood that findings are not idiosyncratic or unreliable.

afterward. Or, in the case of the tracking example above, a study based on statistical information from multiple years would be more credible than a study based on a single year, since only multiple years of data can demonstrate a long-term pattern.

And yet while it is imperative to collect sufficient, appropriate data, at the same time researchers must be careful not to collect everything they possibly can. Instead, they need to choose thoughtfully among the multiple possibilities detailed below. Data analysis is a complex and time-consuming task, and the researcher who collects more data than she has the capacity to analyze is likely either to leave the study unfinished or to confront the painful task of eliminating some data from the study after taking the time and trouble to collect it.

Sources of Data

A wide variety of sources can provide information for an interpretive study. As noted above, researchers often combine multiple sources (triangulation) to increase credibility, or trustworthiness, of their work. In some cases, the data already exist, and the researcher needs only a plan to collect it: policy documents, student work, statistical data, and so on. In others, the researcher generates new data relevant to the research question through such means as interviews and surveys. The following survey presents an overview of typical data sources and collection methods.

Documents and artifacts

The world of education generates a world of paper: lesson plans, curricula, student newspapers, daily bulletins, student records, policies, student handbooks, book lists, report cards, class notes, bulletin board postings, student and personnel records, minutes of meetings, agendas, rules, statistical reports.... Such documents, or **artifacts** of everyday experience, can provide information about what has been encouraged or discouraged, rewarded or punished; about what has happened or will happen; about what has gone unnoticed and unremarked or been publicly trumpeted; about what people thought and said at a given moment in a particular circumstance. Many informative documents are readily available, or permission to access them can be readily obtained.

Artifact

an object created by a person. In educational research, the term *artifact* often refers to samples of student work, such as essays, exams, or notes, or such school documents as handbooks, daily bulletins, and meeting minutes.

With sensitivity to the need for permission to use them (as discussed in Chapter 3), samples of student work can also be informative. Essays, exams, notes, drawings and other work created by students can offer insight into their interests, growth, difficulties, feelings, and engagement. Artifacts are particularly useful because they are recorded bits of ongoing experience; their potential drawback, however, is that it is usually necessary to make copies of originals, and so including them as a data source can require substantive time, effort, and possibly money for photocopying.

Researchers can also ask participants to create objects specifically for the study. For example, many educators are familiar with the strategy of asking people in a group to draw a personal coat-of-arms depicting what they value most. The resulting drawing makes visible and efficiently summarizes the creator's thinking; as this example demonstrates, a well-designed drawing task can serve as potentially useful and efficient research tool. The basic strategy can be adapted in countless ways. A researcher might, for example, ask children to draw a picture of themselves doing homework. The results would be likely to indicate something about the student's feelings (through facial expression) and habits (through the presence or absence of a television or other people). As the child explained the drawing, the researcher might take notes on the meaning for later reference. Or, a researcher might ask a participant to create a bit of writing instead of, or in addition to, a drawing. To supplement the homework drawing, for example, the researcher might ask participants to complete a piece of **freewriting,** jotting anything that comes to mind about homework for three to five minutes. Such devices can capture a good bit of information efficiently.

Freewriting
writing whatever comes to mind, in any form, for a specified time period.

Journals

Although the popularity of journals in college courses has left many practitioners feeling "journaled out," many practitioners find them a useful tool to capture events from everyday professional life. Those who do make them part of a daily routine, often at the day's beginning or end. Entries may include anecdotes, reflections, questions and analyses which have caught the writer's attention—a student's first success, a wondering whether some policy is having unintended effects, questions about or tentative

explanation for why something happened. Such reflective journals can prove a rich source of information during a study. They can trigger the memory of a particularly telling event, or document when an issue first came to a researcher's attention, or illustrate the researcher's change in thinking over time. Capturing bits of experience on paper can be extremely useful in developing understanding of an issue. A look back through a body of such daily entries can illuminate patterns that slip by unnoticed as hectic day follows hectic day.

Alternatively, a researcher who does not normally keep a journal can choose to keep one for the purposes of a particular study. For example, I once asked teachers to help me with a study by keeping a journal specifically on the topic of homework in their classrooms. Several times a week, they recorded any relevant thoughts or experiences, including what kind of homework they had assigned, why, whether students completed it, what they said and how they felt about it, what the teachers themselves said and felt. By the time I was ready to begin analyzing data, each journal provided extensive information on how homework was experienced by both students and teachers.

Or, researchers can keep dialogue journals, in which a left-hand column contains factual material, like events, while a right-hand column is reserved for the researcher's thoughts and comments. This format can offer useful reminders not only of what happened but of what the researcher thought about it at the time.

Field notes

Field notes

a written record of events or observations made by a researcher, often as events occur "in the field"—that is, at a study site (classroom, playground, etc.).

Many researchers like to take notes as events unfold—generally referred to as **field notes**. Immediacy often helps preserve accuracy. For example, it is easier to capture dialogue immediately after it occurs than to try to reconstruct it from memory later. Since memory can be fleeting, notes taken as events unfold can be invaluable in accurately reconstructing events later. There is no universal way for capturing such information; most novices find it necessary to experiment with a variety of methods and materials before settling on a recording method that suits them. Possibilities are as varied as researchers themselves: notebooks, Post-it notes, index cards, stickers, clipboards—anything the researcher can keep at hand and collect easily.

Since action researchers often have to maintain their professional responsibilities (teaching a class, for example) while simultaneously taking notes, they sometimes develop unique forms to make recording and organizing information easier. For example, when some teachers agreed to participate in a study with me and to record spontaneous skills lessons in their elementary classrooms, we developed a check sheet to make their task easier. We listed the skills we thought were most likely to be taught and included columns to indicate whether the lesson was taught to an individual child, a small group, or the whole class. Once a sheet was dated, the teacher needed only to remember to put a single check mark in the appropriate row and column to indicate what was taught and in what format; later, these simple check marks allowed us to tally daily lessons and compare them to the district curriculum. Trying to take notes while concurrently performing professionally can be a challenge, but designing such aids to note-taking can make the process manageable.

Note-taking can be structured in other ways, depending upon the topic and purpose of a particular study. Holly et al. (2005) offer the following list and explanation of field note categories:

- Running record—recording regularly occurring events such as attendance.
- Time intervals—recording what is happening at regular intervals, such as quickly "sweeping" the classroom every 5 minutes to see what kinds of conversations students are having during computer time.
- Specified events—recording every time a specified event occurs, such as students asking questions of their peers during discussion (as opposed to asking the teacher).
- Critical incident—recording moments that seem to be pivotal points in a study, such as the moment a teacher realizes that it is only the male students who are objecting to reading a particular novel, not the entire class.
- Anecdotal record—recording incidents that show growth over time.

Such specific strategies help researchers target the data they collect, minimizing the problem of collecting data that later proves of little or no use.

Interviews and focus groups

Interviews. Researchers who want to know what others think about a topic have an obvious option: ask them. In many circumstances the people directly involved in a situation can and do provide the most reliable information available. Therefore, during planning, researchers can benefit from consciously considering whether they should plan to talk with people who have direct experience relevant to their research questions. For example, researchers studying tracking might decide to talk to the students affected by it. The specific research question to be answered will help answer questions about *which* students, or others, to talk with. For example, if a question focused on tracking in general, then researchers might interview some students from each track to learn about the range of student experiences. If, however, a question asked only how well tracking served gifted students, then interviews would obviously be held only with students from the gifted track.

A complication of interviewing, however, is that people aren't always willing to speak truthfully. It's difficult, for example, to imagine a student readily admitting illegal drug use to a principal during a research interview. While researchers routinely promise subjects anonymity and other protections, such reassurance isn't always effective. During a project that involved interviewing graduate students, for example, I found that for every three students who initially agreed to an interview with me, only one actually followed through; the others changed their minds because they felt too strongly that telling the truth to a faculty member, any faculty member, was too dangerous.

Research groups can be helpful in such circumstances. When they include members of various stakeholder groups, some members can provide access to certain groups and information that would not be possible otherwise. For example, unlike a principal interviewing a student about drug use, a student interviewer might be able to elicit honest information from a peer. When devising a research plan that includes interviews, researchers should consider not only which persons they would like to interview, but also how likely those persons are to cooperate and to be candid. Who will do the interviewing may be another important question if sensitive issues are involved.

Like other methodologies, interviews take a variety of forms. They can be conducted with a single person,

which may encourage some people to speak more freely, or in groups, which can provoke a kind of creative synergy when a comment from one person sparks a entirely new line of thought then followed by someone else. **Focus groups**, as their names suggest, are a type of group interview in which researchers bring a representative group of people together to focus on their perceptions of a particular issue or event. They are useful for accessing a broad range of opinions on a single topic within a single session. Television networks, for example, often convene focus groups of local citizens to watch a political debate and then discuss their varied reactions to it. In a school setting, focus groups of representative students, parents, and teachers might be convened to explore a question like "What advantages and disadvantages do you see in adopting a uniform policy?" A focus group's main advantage is its efficiency in eliciting a range of opinions in a limited amount of time.

No matter its format, any interview can be **structured**, **semi-structured**, or **unstructured**, depending upon the researcher's purpose. A researcher might ask only pre-determined questions in a structured interview to ensure that her specific questions are answered, a useful and efficient strategy when the researcher is clear about exactly what she wants to know. However, less structured interviews hold the possibility of expanding the researcher's thinking; given free rein to shape the conversation, a participant following his own line of thinking may open a new perspective the researcher hadn't considered.

Some words of caution apply to all interview situations. As is true for research questions, the researcher should craft questions carefully to avoid wording that might influence a subject's thinking or answer. For example, the question "Would you agree that this policy is depriving our schools of desperately needed resources?" calls for a very different response than "Do you have any thoughts on how this policy has affected schools?" The first question intends to elicit agreement with the interviewer's position; the second more genuinely seeks information on the participant's thinking. The wording of questions is so significant that most often, interview questions are included as part of a written research report so that the reader can judge whether or not they were likely to have influenced participants' responses.

Focus group

a form of group interview in which representative persons are brought together to explore their various thoughts on a specific topic.

Semi-structured interview

An interview in which the researcher asks some predetermined questions but also allows interviewees time and opportunity to explore other areas they think relevant

---

Structured interview

An interview limited to questions the researcher formulated before the interview begins.

Unstructured interview

An interview where the researcher asks only very broad questions that allow the interviewee to substantively determine topics of discussion.

Also, it is worth keeping in mind the common saying that "something was lost in translation." When researchers take notes rather than audiotape interviews, the notes reflect what the researcher thinks she heard—which is to say, they may or may not be accurate. Everyone has had the experience of someone else being sure that we said something we are sure we did *not* say. If the record of an interview is to be the interviewer's notes, it is a good idea to check accuracy with the subject, either during or at the end of the interview. This is easily done by saying something like "Let me just check and be sure I've heard and understood you correctly. According to my notes, you said...." Misrepresenting what was said during an interview, accidentally or otherwise, is not only grossly unfair to the interviewee but also something that can cost the researcher precious trust and access to other subjects in the future.

Good interviewing involves strategy and practice, but textbooks and many other research materials (including several listed in the Resources section) offer readily accessible and detailed advice.

Surveys

Surveys are an efficient way to gather larger amounts of data on what participants think, but like other methods, they have their drawbacks. Sometimes, persuading people to actually complete a survey can be difficult because they receive so many requests. A reality is that the shorter a survey form, the more likely it is to be completed. Obviously, however, keeping surveys short means including only a few questions, resulting in limited information collected. Also, if a survey question happens to be worded poorly, then the results are meaningless. For example, the question "Have you helped a community agency recently?" is open to wide interpretation that would likely muddle results. One participant may say yes, assuming that "helped" includes having donated money to the United Way; another might say yes because six months ago, he donated used computers to the Boy Scouts (which are a community group, but not a community agency); another might say yes because a year ago, she had spent ten hours every week working at a soup kitchen. Because words like "helped," "agency," and "recently" are open to such varied interpretation, it would be impossible to say what a "yes" in answer to this ques-

tion might actually mean. An interview participant can always ask "What do you mean by recently?" but with no researcher nearby to provide such clarification, survey questions must be particularly exact. Ideally, a researcher tries out a draft survey with a few willing people before beginning data collection, asking them to identify places where they think the questions are unclear or open to multiple interpretations. It is a rare survey that isn't significantly improved by such a trial run.

A related question is who should be asked to complete surveys. One group? More than one group? All group members? Some group members? How will people or groups be chosen? If there are multiple groups, will it be important to be able to break out responses for each subgroup? Does that mean forms will need to be coded in some way? Again, carefully planning well in advance is in order. The researcher uses the study's questions to help determine the audience/s most likely to provide credible and relevant information and to think through how it may later be necessary to group responses in some way (students/teachers, for example, or junior high/high school students).

If participants are likely to have ready access to the Worldwide Web, action researchers interested in surveys might want to explore free online survey sites. Some, like Survey Monkey.com (http://www.surveymonkey.com/), allow anyone to log on and design a survey, using either its prewritten questions or the researcher's own. This site, like others, allows for multiple question format, including multiple choice and open-ended text. Moreover, the Survey Monkey site will host the survey and generate reports based on responses. Such free tools can make surveying attractively easy and efficient for researchers. As noted in the Resources section, StatPac, Inc. offers a free, online survey tutorial that is useful, even if not specifically intended for educators (http://www.statpac.com/surveys/).

Audiotapes, videotapes, photos

Researchers can also use audiotapes, videotapes and photographs to capture daily events. Each has its own benefits and limitations. Although both audiotapes and videotapes can make participants self-conscious at first, many report quickly forgetting that they were being recording. Assuming audiotape quality is good—something the researcher must ensure—exact words can be documented,

as well as such other features as pauses and emphases. The same is true for videotapes, which offer additional information on context, body language, facial expression, and so on. The great challenge associated with both taping methods is that of extracting data from the medium.

It can take hours to watch and/or listen to tapes and videos repeatedly during analysis, so for efficiency both kinds of recordings are often transcribed into written form. However, transcription can be expensive and can require considerable expertise if nuances in the originals are to be retained. The person transcribing must use written symbols to indicate significant changes in volume, tone, emphasis, and so on. A person transcribing a videotape might, for example, have to decide whether to describe a particular facial expression as a *smile* or a *smirk*. In making such decisions, the transcriber assigns meaning to the original data, potentially affecting both the findings and the trustworthiness of the study. The problem of extracting data is exacerbated when, as frequently happens, researchers collect more data than they need. In this case, they must either find resources to transcribe everything, or spend time prescreening recordings to select for transcription the most informative material in the mass collected.

Much more efficient is for researchers to consider the costs of transcription as they plan and to collect and transcribe only a manageable amount of data. Ideally, they would then work with both the original recording and the transcription. In practice, however, researchers may lack time or funds for extensive transcription and so they work primarily with original recordings, with little or none of the material transcribed. This is particularly true for studies limited in scope and distribution, as action research studies often are. This is a feasible strategy, but it means that the amount of data to be so analyzed will need to be fairly limited.

Though perhaps less commonly used, photographs can also be useful. If a group wanted to investigate safety issues at school bus stops, for example, photography might be a good tool. Photos of each bus stop could be taken daily, perhaps at five-minute intervals over a twenty-minute time span, for one week. Together, the pictures would reveal conditions at each stop on a typical day: how many children were waiting, whether an adult was supervising them, how much traffic was in the area, and so on. Of course, the

same information might be recorded in notes, but photographs would likely be easier to compile and more persuasive as evidence.

While this overview includes the most common means of data collection, it is not exhaustive. Unique research questions can lead the researcher to design unique methods. This is fine. The ultimate test of any methodology is whether it can be implemented in ways that suit the researcher and that will reliably yield credible information.

Analyzing Data

Data analysis
the process of deciding what new information the collected data provide. During the analysis process, researchers sift through the data looking for patterns or themes. Data analysis yields the researcher's findings.

For many researchers, the most exciting—as well as the most frustrating—segment of the research process is **data analysis**. Once all of the data is collected, often filling boxes or shelves or crates to overflowing, inexperienced researchers can feel at a loss, confronting a mountain of information with no idea how to begin tunneling through it. While many strategies exist to begin chipping an opening that will lead somewhere into the mountain, the most important factors are the researchers' time, patience and faith.

An Overview of the Analysis Process

Dana and Yendol-Silva (2003) offer a particularly apt metaphor for the data analysis process. Imagine, they suggest, being faced with the task of putting a jigsaw puzzle together under unusual conditions. The pieces come in a bag, not a box, so there's no picture to guide the effort. Moreover, there are extra pieces in the bag that won't fit into the final product. Still, even without knowing what the pieces will add up to or which ones don't belong, beginning steps are possible. Pieces can be sorted by color, and at least some within each color group will begin to fit together. As small puzzle segments begin taking shape, pieces originally placed in the wrong color group (that's not sky, it's water!) are moved to the correct one as key differences and similarities among groups become increasingly clear. Eventually, the frame is in place; isolated segments begin to fit together; superfluous pieces are excluded, and the last piece finally locks into place (p. 91). The formless chaos of the beginning is eventually resolved into an intelligible picture. Such is also the experience of researchers,

who begin with a jumbled mass of detailed information and work steadily to organize the discrete bits into a meaningful whole. It might not produce the picture they were after when they wrote their original research question, but it will produce a picture.

In this process, it's important that the researcher not overreact to the beginning chaos of **raw data**, which can intimidate even the most experienced researchers: "The murkiness of data analysis is what scares any researcher.…there is a fair amount of uncertainness in the task" (Hubbard & Power, 1999, p. 117). Nothing may be more disheartening than having spent weeks or months collecting data and then having the fear that it will never make sense, that nothing useful can or will ever come of it. So common is this feeling during early data analysis that many practical guides emphasize, as this text is emphasizing, that feeling overwhelmed at first is a normal part of the analysis process. Fear is normal. Uncertainty is normal. Novice researchers, like experienced researchers, move past it by trusting that patience and perseverance will reliably help them move from unfocused preliminary sorting to the point where segments of the data begin to click together meaningfully.

Raw data
data, or information, collected in a research study before it has been analyzed or organized in any way. A common metaphor contrasts raw data with *cooked* data, or data that has been summarized or organized in some fashion.

Preliminary Analysis Strategies

Beginning during data collection

The uncertainty stage can be made a bit easier if some preliminary data analysis is built into data collection. For example, there is no need to wait several weeks before beginning to analyze data that is collected daily. Instead, the researcher might review data weekly, writing summaries and notes identifying the week's most striking information and possible emerging patterns. Later analysis can then begin with a review of weekly summaries, which are likely to suggest places to begin looking more closely for patterns or themes. In addition, there is the possibility that preliminary analysis as data collection is in progress will suggest an additional question to ask or demonstrate that a particular question is being misinterpreted. For a variety of reasons, then, doing some preliminary analysis during data collection can be helpful.

Another possibility during data collection is for the researcher to create and maintain an **index** to the data and/

Index
a guide to the location of information on a specific topic in a large body of material—in a book, or in a set of research notes, for example.

or notes as various topics appear. For example, if student writing were being collected and the researcher noted several references to parents, one index entry might read "Parents: John: June 8 (p. 3), June 10 (p. 1); Jenny: June 15 (p. 2)" and so on. Similar entries could be created for other groups or for any topic or category—homework, behavior, Jonathan, class activities, or whatever. Such an index allows the researcher to begin by reviewing all data on one topic, and it facilitates later comparison and contrast of different areas. (Did parents and students voice the same concerns? Did Jonathan's behavior in class vary with the class activity?) While the index entries may not correlate to later categories of analysis, they at least offer the researcher an organized way to begin reviewing the mass of data collected.

Note-taking forms and other data collection tools can also have starting points for analysis built into them. Suppose, for example, that three different groups had completed a survey. Survey forms might include information that would facilitate different kinds of comparisons later on. For example, a check box on the form for the participant to indicate his or her role (student; teacher; administrator; parent) would allow the researcher to sort responses into groups and compare what various groups said. Or, asking for such information as grade averages from students might allow for useful intra-group comparisons. Although it's not always possible to say ahead of time what comparisons may be useful, having the option of examining information in an organized way can help the researcher approach what may otherwise appear a fairly chaotic collection of detail. Confidentiality is important, but it is possible to code forms in ways that protect confidentiality yet still provide the researcher with enough information to compare responses from various groups.

Starting with no starting point

It often happens, however, that the researcher had no way to do preliminary analysis during data collection and can see no way to impose any beginning organizational strategy (a monochromatic puzzle!). In that case, only one strategy is possible (though it is reliably productive): begin. Simply begin. As the person trying to put the monochromatic pieces together has no option except to spread them out and just keep looking at them until some differences

emerge, the researcher has no option but to begin reading (or viewing, or listening to) the data. And then to do it again. And again, as many times as necessary until a path forward gradually appears.

There is no need for researchers to worry about what the data may mean during a first reading. Instead, the first task is simply to become familiar with all of the many pages of information that have been collected. There is no way for the researcher to begin connecting the disjointed pieces of information without becoming thoroughly familiar with what the data as a whole contains. Once familiar with what has been collected, the researcher's next step may be to reread yet again, writing a description of what appears while rereading. For example, "June 6: report of difficult conference with parents about Len's frequent absences and an account of a successful lesson on long division." Sometimes distilling the data into such descriptions makes the detail more manageable. As descriptions increase, the researcher may begin to notice certain kinds of reports that come up over and over again (notes about disciplinary issues, or about a particular child, or about successful lessons). Such repetition indicates good places for the researcher to begin looking more closely.

Or, a researcher might extend descriptions of the data by adding to it comments on any surprises it may contain. What was expected but doesn't appear? What appears unexpectedly? For example, a research group might survey a community about perceived discrimination and find that descriptions of the data frequently note anecdotes about race, gender, ability and age discrimination. Since discrimination based on sexual orientation is common, its absence would be surprising. Thus, thorough descriptions of data include observations not only about what does appear but about what doesn't. Researchers can later consider whether they think the absence is significant. Perhaps not. On the other hand, perhaps they will decide that the silence may indicate that gay members of the community avoid calling attention to themselves, even anonymously, because the community climate is so hostile. Good data description will point out such surprises so that researchers later can examine them thoughtfully, as they complete a later, full analysis of the data.

Categories, Coding and Findings

The point of all analysis is to identify patterns in the data, to see what may be common in the experiences or thinking recorded. To begin identifying patterns, researchers often move from describing the data to asking questions about it: Did something happen over and over again? Did the same complaints or concerns surface repeatedly? Did anything, any trend, seem to strengthen or weaken over time? What behaviors, events or language were typical? Atypical? How did the participants seem to feel about the topic, the researcher, each other? Why? What specific words did participants most frequently use? Such questioning is known as **interrogating the data**: asking questions of the information as a way to make sense of it.

Interrogating the data
asking questions of the information collected as a way to make sense of it. For example, "Do opinions seem the same for all members of each group, or do members of each group have widely varied opinions?"

Common categories

Patterns can take shape in many categories: events, issues, trends, behaviors, feelings, word use...any area of experience. While individual researchers may certainly identify idiosyncratic categories and patterns, some categories commonly prove useful in trying to make sense of data. Following is a brief list of some of the most common with sample questions demonstrating how the category might be useful in interrogating the data (adapted from Dana & Yendol-Silva, 2003).

Time. Do data reflect differences related to time of day, or day of the week, or other time variable? Do any of these things appear to happen simultaneously? Do they seem to happen in a predictable sequence? Do the perceptions reported in the data seem stable over time, or do they vary significantly at particular moments?

Issues. How do various groups' definition of this issue vary? Which issues appear most and least frequently? Do the many minor complaints suggest a single larger issue?

Roles. Do participants in different roles seem to share the same perceptions, or are perceptions varied even among those in the same roles? Did participants appear to assume different roles at different times? How do participants define their role in creating and solving this problem?

Behaviors. What behaviors are most commonly reported? Is there any evidence that some particular thing generates (or inhibits) particular behaviors? How do different groups define and perceive this behavior?

Relationships. What different relationships exist among these participants? To what extent are participants' relationships stable? Which alliances among individual members of this group seem to impede consensus, and which facilitate it?

Strategies. What strategies did participants use to reach their objectives? What strategies seemed most useful to participants, which least useful? What intended effects did this strategy produce, and what unintended effects?

Emotions. How do participants seem to feel about these events or issues? What emotions appear to have prompted these actions? What factors prompted the intense resistance evident in participants' early responses? What factors appear to have lessened resistance? What impact have these events had on how participants feel about themselves?

Meanings. In what ways were the meanings that participants assigned to the same event similar and/or different? What prior experiences did participants refer to when explaining why they assigned a particular meaning to an event?

Settings. Do the behaviors reported seem to correlate with particular settings or conditions? How might the configuration of the room have affected interpersonal relationships that developed within it? How often did participants refer to setting when discussing events, and what did they say?

Of course, none of these categories is mutually excusive. Each is simply a lens to use in viewing the data now this way, now that, until a larger picture begins to come into focus. When a first set of patterns appear—because the first set may, like other elements of the process, evolve over time—the researcher moves onto coding.

Coding

After identifying an initial set of categories to sort data into (administrator/student/teacher responses, or supportive/neutral/hostile comments, for example), a researcher's next step is to create and record clear definitions for each category. This is another task that sounds simplistic, but is both necessary and important because over time and with the researcher's immersion in detail, categories have a nasty way of becoming murky. A category that seems fully self-explanatory at the beginning of sorting

data—like "unhelpful behaviors"—may become cloudy later. For example, suppose data indicate that one student never asks the teacher for help: is that an "unhelpful" behavior, because the student might complete the task more efficiently with help? Or, is it actually an instance of a student's willingness to persevere that is helping him develop self-confidence and independence—a "helpful" behavior?

Clearly defining each category before beginning data sorting can help avoid such tangles. In this case, for example, much better to provide a definition of the category before beginning: "Unhelpful behavior: a behavior that prevents a student from successfully completing an assigned task." With this criteria, the researcher would be able to tell how to categorize the behavior based on whether or not the student was successful in completing the assigned work. Fine tuning such descriptions can take time (Must a student really complete the work for a behavior to be successful, or would it be enough for the student to make significant independent progress on it?) Experience is likely to lead the researcher to revise categories even as sorting progresses, but it is nevertheless a good strategy to eliminate as much ambiguity from categories as possible before beginning; taking time to write careful descriptions can save significant time and trouble later.

Once categories have been defined as well as possible, the researcher is ready to begin aggregating individual bits of information into groups, or categories. This is done by **coding** the data—that is, by developing a system to identify particular pieces as belonging to particular categories. Many systems are possible, and all researchers select strategies that they are comfortable with and that suit their particular purposes. Color coding is common; each category is assigned a different color, and individual bits of data are marked with the appropriate color. A researcher can then pick out individual bits of information that seem to fit together simply by glancing at the colors on a page. If text is in electronic form, the text-highlighting feature can make color coding very easy. Alternatively, a researcher might develop a symbol system instead. For example, a bit of text might be marked with a plus sign for positive behaviors, a minus sign for negative behaviors, or a check for a behavior that seems neither. Any coding system—color, symbol, drawing or any other—that helps the reader

Coding

a system to identify individual pieces of data as belonging to a particular category. For example, a researcher might highlight classroom anecdotes relating to writing with yellow; relating to reading with blue; and relating to math with green.

immediately recognize a piece of information as belonging to a particular category is fine.

If coding seems too cumbersome in some cases, the researcher has the option of simply sorting the data physically—into piles on the floor, into different folders or envelopes or boxes. An electronic version of this strategy is to compile a word processing file for each category. Some researchers literally cut up copies of the data (never, ever the originals) and sort individual bits, like playing cards, into piles of things that seem to be related, shuffling and reshuffling individual bits until they are satisfied that everything fits well where it's been placed—or until they can revise categories satisfactorily to accommodate all of the information. Similar reshuffling can be accomplished with a cut and paste feature in a word processing program. As is true in other elements of the process: any system that works for the researcher's purposes is a fine system.

Findings

Findings
statements of what a researcher has learned from data analysis. For example, after data analysis, a researcher may find "Students typically offer one of two explanations for why they failed a test: lack of studying or test anxiety."

Once researchers are satisfied that data has been sorted into meaningful categories, they can begin to formulate **findings**—statements about the information contained in the data. Data analysis asks questions of information collected: "Which strategies did participants find useful?" "How did members of different groups explain the problem?" Findings provide such answers as: "Participants found two strategies particularly useful: freewriting and concept mapping." "Each participant group explained the low test scores differently: teachers felt that students simply weren't working hard enough, while students felt that teachers rushed them through the material without allowing them enough time to master it."

Any finding must be based on specific information in the data. The researcher should always be able to answer the question "Why do you say that?" by citing specific supporting evidence from the information collected. For example, to support the finding that participants valued freewriting and concept mapping, a researcher might include in a written report several positive comments from interviews.

Making Meaning: Theorizing

The most intriguing phase of the research process for most researchers is moving from findings to interpreta-

Theorizing

offering interpretations of the findings; explaining what the researcher believes the findings *mean*. For example, in a study that found that many students had difficulty reading college texts, a researcher might theorize that they had received insufficient reading instruction and practice.

tion—a process sometimes called **theorizing** in descriptions of action research. For example, a finding might be: "Fridays consistently had the lowest rates of student attendance." The researcher might offer these interpretations or explanations: "Such absences may be due to students' frequent weekend travel or to teachers having adjusted to the absences by doing little in Friday classes, thus reducing incentives for Friday attendance." Another way of thinking about theorizing is to think of it as answering the question "What does this finding *mean?*" "It might mean that students skip Fridays to extend frequent weekends away, and/or that professors have gotten into the habit of doing little in Friday classes because of frequent absences—encouraging still more class cutting."

It is important to note that the point of theorizing is not to formulate AN interpretation of the findings—not to provide a single, "correct" interpretation. Action research is, after all, interpretivist research, which assumes that all knowledge is socially constructed, and that any reading of the world (including any reading of research findings) is only one of many possible readings. It is important, then, that the researcher approach this task without the burden of feeling it necessary to *prove* something true beyond any doubt. Instead, action researchers offer interpretations they consider most likely, using their own experiences and perspectives to inform their judgments.

Suppose, for example, a researcher conducted a study asking about the causes of low test scores and found that teachers and students disagreed about what caused them, with teachers saying students didn't work hard enough and students saying that teachers' expectations were too stringent. The same findings might well lead different researchers in different schools to very different interpretations.

For example, a researcher might have conducted this study in an affluent high school, where students spend many after-school hours in extracurricular activities to increase the chances they will be accepted to an elite college. The college preparatory academic work might also be rigorous to help students prepare for college entrance exams and other academic challenges ahead. The researcher familiar with the school might be aware that students often find themselves caught between the high expectations of both teachers and extracurricular supervisors (coaches, club advisors). In this case, the researcher might theorize

that "This study suggests that students cannot meet the high expectations for time commitments of both academic and extracurricular authorities."

But suppose the same study were conducted in a poor school with a high dropout rate. It is unfortunate but true that many teachers have stereotypical ideas about cultures they are not familiar with, and so teachers' assumption that students don't work hard might indicate a prevailing stereotype that students from certain cultural groups are inherently lazy. A researcher might be aware not only of those stereotypes but also of the fact that students frequently lack the basic skills necessary to do assigned work; many might have stopped attempting any work if their past efforts were consistently fruitless and frustrating. The researcher's theorizing in this case might look very different: "The finding suggests that teachers may have a stereotypical sense of all students as lazy as well as an inaccurate impression of their current abilities; students may have stopped believing they can succeed at school or that anyone cares whether or not they do."

The meaning assigned to the same findings in each case (teachers think students don't work/students think work is inappropriate) can be, as illustrated above, drastically different, depending upon the unique perspective each researcher brings to a study. It is in interpreting, or theorizing about, the findings that researchers rely most heavily on their intimate knowledge of the research context.

No, This Doesn't Mean Anything Goes

A common complaint about action research is that it isn't reliable: there's no way to tell if the researcher's findings and theorizing are "right" or not. As noted above, and repeatedly in the earlier chapters of this book, interpretivist research never seeks a "right" answer because there are none—only interpretations. Many people jump from that assertion to the conclusion that one study is as good as another and that anyone can say anything and call it "research."

Such people are uninformed.

Without attempting to be "right," action researchers can and do take steps to enhance the credibility of their work. Some of the most common include checking for commonalities *and* anomalies in the data and asking for feedback on analysis and interpretation.

Attending to similarities and differences in the data

Triangulation. Triangulation has already been mentioned in relation to data sources, where it was suggested that multiple (at least three) different sources would help strengthen the study. Similarly, when the same finding is evident in three different areas of data analysis, the finding is obviously strengthened. For example, if three groups (teachers, students and administrators) each indicated disrespect as a problem in a school, then the finding is stronger than if only one group had said so. Or, perhaps three different data sources (surveys, interviews, and disciplinary records) might have indicated it as a problem, again making the finding stronger than if only one source had done so. Or, three different researchers might independently analyze the same data and reach the same conclusions (assign the same grade to the same paper or assign individual pieces of evidence to the same categories). Triangulation is simply a sophisticated way of naming the common sense principle that the more evidence there is to support a finding, the more credible the finding.

Negative case analysis

searching the data for instances that don't fit or that contradict emerging findings; discussion of negative cases strengthens the trustworthiness of a study.

Negative case analysis. Negative case analysis is a similarly sophisticated way of naming the very good idea of looking for contradictions in the data—for identifying exceptions to findings and thinking about what they might mean. To return to the example above, suppose that students and teachers had overwhelmingly named disrespect as a problem, but it never came up in data collected from administrators. What might that mean? That teachers and students were routinely disrespectful of each other but not administrators? That administrators didn't consider the same behaviors disrespectful that teachers and students did? That administrators were aware of the disrespect, but being more familiar with disciplinary issues, didn't bother to mention it because of their far greater concern with larger issues like inadequate funding and difficulties in ensuring student safety? In some instances, analyzing an apparent contradiction may lead to a more accurately phrased finding ("For teachers and students, disrespect was a significant concern; administrators, on the other hand, were most concerned about the larger practical issues of funding and student safety.") In many other instances, such discrepancy might motivate the researcher to collect more data to clarify the issue—perhaps interviewing a few administrators about their concerns.

No researcher is required to provide an explanation for every anomaly in the data, but discussing exceptions and contractions in a report of the study (with or without possible explanations) enhances the credibility of the study by making clear the researcher has tried to be thorough and forthright in reporting on the evidence.

Peer debriefing and member checks

At some point, either during or after analysis, action researchers generally ask others to respond to their first interpretations of the data. Most often they consult their peers—**peer debriefing**—or the study's participants—**member checks** (Lincoln and Guba, 1985). Two points make such checking important.

First, every researcher becomes so immersed in a study during data analysis that it becomes difficult to see the data in any way other than as fitting into the constructed categories. An experienced peer unfamiliar with the data can provide a fresh perspective and point out questions, anomalies, weak or missing evidence, or other gaps in the work; she can also provide valuable confirmation that the analysis and interpretation seem feasible as well. A teacher doing an action research study might share what he's found with a supportive colleague and ask for feedback on whether the findings and interpretation seem likely. Researchers can have conversations with colleagues or circulate drafts of written reports (more on that in the next chapter); feedback might be verbal or written, formal or informal. No matter the form, the insights that feedback provides allow the researcher to consider possible gaps or misreadings in the initial analysis, make revisions, and improve the trustworthiness of the study.

Second, it is important to remember that action research does not involve studies *on* participants (as in positivist human subjects research). Instead, it involves studies *with* participants. Therefore, participants should be among those invited to comment on the researcher's analysis. Only participants' direct involvement can ensure that the work fairly and accurately represents their viewpoints and experiences. In addition to contributing to the trustworthiness of the study, giving participants a real voice equalizes power arrangements by making them true partners in the research process; it upsets the expert researcher/dependent practitioner relationship as many

Peer debriefing

the process of a researcher sharing preliminary data analysis and interpretation with a peer, or colleague, to determine whether he or she finds the researcher's analysis credible or convincing. Peer debriefing strengthens the trustworthiness of a study.

Member checks/ Member validation

the process of a researcher sharing preliminary data analysis and interpretation with study participants to determine whether they agree or disagree with the researcher's analysis. Member checks enhance the trustworthiness of a study.

proponents of action research intend. While it may take more time and trouble for a group to reach consensus about what the data mean, the process deepens understanding for everyone involved and fosters widespread support for resulting action plans.

Researchers should understand that giving participants a real voice in formulating study findings and implications can result in tensions and ethical dilemmas. What if the researcher's analysis is radically different from the participants'? What if both researcher and participants feel strongly their analysis is correct? There are no easy answers: any democratic project can result in such struggles, which need to be worked out through some kind of negotiation. Perhaps both perspectives need to be presented in some way, and those who hear or read about the study will have to decide for themselves which interpretation seems more likely—or what else the disagreement might mean. Again, since interpretivist research seeks no single right answer, disagreement is not fatal to the work. Even disagreement can advance understanding by illustrating two different interpretations of the same situation.

When researchers feel comfortable with their findings and the meanings they assign to them, they can move on to considering what they suggest in terms of action.

GLOSSARY

Artifact: an object created by a person. In educational research, the term *artifact* often refers to samples of student work, such as essays, exams, or notes, or such school documents as handbooks, daily bulletins, and meeting minutes.

Coding: a system to identify individual pieces of data as belonging to a particular category. For example, a researcher might highlight classroom anecdotes relating to writing with yellow; relating to reading with blue; and relating to math with green.

Data analysis: the process of deciding what new information the collected data provide. During the analysis process, researchers sift through the data looking for patterns or themes. Data analysis yields the researcher's findings.

Field notes: a written record of events or observations made by a researcher, often as events occur "in the field"—that is, at a study site (classroom, playground, etc.).

Findings: statements of what a researcher has learned from data analysis. For example, after data analysis, a researcher may find "Students typically offer one of two explanations for why they failed a test: lack of studying or test anxiety."

Focus group: a form of group interview in which representative persons are brought together to explore their various thoughts on a specific topic.

Freewriting: writing whatever comes to mind, in any form, for a specified time period.

Index: a guide to the location of information on a specific topic in a large body of material—in a book, or in a set of research notes, for example.

Interrogating the data: asking questions of the information collected as a way to make sense of it. For example, "Do opinions seem the same for all members of each group, or do members of each group have widely varied opinions?"

Member checks/Member validation: the process of a researcher sharing preliminary data analysis and interpretation with study participants to determine whether they agree or disagree with the researcher's analysis. Member checks enhance the trustworthiness of a study.

Negative case analysis: searching the data for instances that don't fit or that contradict emerging findings; discussion of negative cases strengthens the trustworthiness of a study.

Peer debriefing: the process of a researcher sharing preliminary data analysis and interpretation with a peer, or colleague, to determine whether he or she finds the researcher's analysis credible or convincing. Peer debriefing strengthens the trust-worthiness of a study.

Raw data: data, or information, collected in a research study before it has been analyzed or organized in any way. A common metaphor contrasts raw data with *cooked* data, or data that has been summarized or organized in some fashion.

Semi-structured interview: An interview in which the researcher asks some predetermined questions but also allows intervie-wees time and opportunity to explore other areas they think relevant

Structured interview: An interview limited to questions the researcher formulated before the interview begins.

Theorizing: offering interpretations of the findings; explaining what the researcher believes the findings *mean*. For example, in a study that found that many students had difficulty reading college texts, a researcher might theorize that they had received insufficient reading instruction and practice.

Triangulation: to collect three different types of data relevant to the same question in order to increase the likelihood that findings are not idiosyncratic or unreliable.

Unstructured interview: An interview where the researcher asks only very broad questions that allow the interviewee to substantively determine topics of discussion.

CHAPTER FIVE

Action Plans, Recording Studies, and Sharing

Action Plans

From Thought to Plan

With all of the information provided by the research process, at this point researchers can say "This is what I know now, and this is how I know it." To move from there to an action plan involves answering the question *Now that I know _____, what seems the logical next step?* For example:

- Now that we know our community is inhospitable to its gay members, we will plan an awareness campaign and create a support network.
- Now that we know student absences are so high in part because so many students stay home to take care of younger siblings, we will contact local and state officials and see if we can't work with them to do something about the availability of low cost daycare.
- Now that we know few students do well on fractions using this text, we will decide whether to change books or develop supplemental materials for all teachers to use. In either case, we need to designate appropriate persons to see that the work gets done.

- Now that we know students suffer physical illness from test stress, as a community we must stop emphasizing to children that the whole school will suffer if they score badly. We also need to devise and publicize suggestions for how we can emphasize learning rather than grades throughout the school.

As these examples demonstrate, the new information that systematic research provides often makes logical action/s obvious. In the above, education is an obvious response to lack of awareness, as supplemental materials or replacement are obvious remedies for a weak text.

Many models suggest that in addition to identifying such interventions, action plans should include launching a new action research project to monitor their effects. Such monitoring is important because actions may or may not achieve the intended objectives, and they can have both intended and unintended consequences. For example, an educational campaign about gay rights might, as intended, raise community awareness of gay rights issues; however, it might also have the unintended consequence of antagonizing other groups who also suffer discrimination and resent the special attention paid to the gay community. A study to monitor effects of the action would likely reveal this new problem and promote a strategy to remedy it. The need to determine exactly what effects change strategies actually have in practice explains why so many theorists describe the action research process as cyclical: each project leads to action, and ideally, each action is monitored after implementation.

New studies also become desirable for reasons other than monitoring. By the time the analysis portion of a study is complete, the process may have sparked ideas for new projects that build on it in other ways. For example, the study above might have triggered a question like "What kinds of community institutions or events (i.e., theater, or orchestra, or youth center) might be designed and successfully implemented as a means of fostering interaction and familiarity among various groups in our community?" Rather than thinking in negative terms of problems, the researcher might begin thinking in proactive terms, considering what actions might avoid problems in the first place. Another example of the same kind of thinking at an institutional level might be "What do we do as a community to signal that every member is welcome and

appreciated here? How inclusive are our artwork, our bulletin boards, our cafeteria menu, and other elements of our physical environment? Where might we do better?"

Or, a new study might be prompted by the fact that the original research question wasn't answered or was answered only in part. For example, researchers who explored the question "What strategies can we implement to help alleviate teacher and student stress born of high stakes testing?" might decide that changing messages to students is a good strategy—but an insufficient one. They might realize that the study just completed explored only local conditions, and not the larger context of the problem. A new study to explore what the school might do to help promote changes in the law creating stressful conditions might also seem a desirable next step.

In short, it's always a good idea to monitor the effects of change strategies, and it's a common phenomenon for one research question to lead to others. These characteristics explain why so many models of action research describe the process as cyclical or spiraling.

Strengthening Action Plans and Outcomes

Adjust planning detail to complexity

If an individual researcher is exploring changes in her own practice, an action plan can be a brief and simple statement of next steps: "I will rework all of my written assignments to give students more choice in topics, and I will begin scheduling conferences to discuss rough drafts." However, studies focusing on larger issues—"What can we do to make every member of our community feel valued?"—might produce a list of possible actions, each of which will require more detailed planning before implementation. For such cases, Stringer (2004) recommends what he calls an "action agenda," which lists actions in order of priority and sorts them into short-term, medium-term, and long-term projects (155). For each item in each category, responsible persons and a time line should be designated. So, for the question above, a priority list might include

- Implement more diversity in the institutional environment (artwork, staff, food, etc.)
- Implement more diversity in curricular offerings

- Arrange more speakers and programs indicating that many cultures are acknowledged and valued by the institution

Obviously, each of these is complex and would take the efforts of several people to implement, with some things (a more diversified cafeteria menu) being relatively easy to implement in the short term and others (a more diversified curriculum) taking much more time and effort to accomplish. Detailing not just what needs to be done but by whom and when can help ensure that a study actually results in some action, not just new but inert information. Action plans work best when the specific people to lead each effort are designated and when various timelines (for first meetings, interim reports, draft plans) are also laid out.

Engage stakeholders

In many cases, the people who will be affected by the actions a study generates will have been involved in the research process and so will already have "bought in" to the process. In other cases, stakeholders will not have been involved—and in these cases, it's important to enlist them to assist in the change process. Few people like to have changes imposed on them without their input, and so it's possible to head off opposition by giving various stakeholders a voice in shaping changes. For example, a school community that decided to implement uniforms despite the fact that some parents and students opposed it might gain greater acceptance for the plan if those opposed are specifically invited to help design uniform guidelines.

Even more importantly, however, inviting stakeholders from various groups into the action implementation process ensures that strategies will be informed by new perspectives that may see some angles unnoticed by the original researchers. It is much better to have stakeholders identify omissions and misperceptions at the beginning of an implementation process where plans can still be adjusted than to learn about mistakes through their anger or resistance later. In short, the more input all stakeholders have into design of a specific action, the more likely it is to be successful.

Recording and Sharing the Study

Although individual practitioners studying their own practice may begin a project with no intention of formally recording it, there are several good reasons to compose a written record—even a brief and informal record. Because there are also good reasons to share the work with a variety of audiences, researchers should not stash a summary of a project away in a drawer without at least considering the many opportunities and formats available to them for sharing. This chapter explains the characteristics typical of written action research reports—which usually bear little resemblance to research articles in journals practitioners may be familiar with. It also overviews alternative formats for presenting findings and the range of outlets available.

An earlier point about action research applies here: modest beginnings often lead to more ambitious projects. A novice researcher undertaking a modest first study just to test the waters of action research might want to build confidence by planning to keep the project a private matter, not sharing at all except for, perhaps, a trusted colleague or two. In small steps forward from there, she can move on to sharing with other colleagues, maybe first in informal conversations or groups during in-service days, and then later in publications or presentations at the local, then state, and then national levels. Only a researcher's ambition and energy limit the boundaries of the work. The more that researchers share their work, however, the more that colleagues—and the profession—will benefit. New and reliable bodies of professional knowledge can come only when researchers freely share their work with each other.

Written Records

Benefits to the researcher

Knowledge not recorded is easily lost, which is the primary reason for writing a summary of a research project. It's often useful to take a look back at what we've done and said and learned earlier, and a written summary of a study can capture information permanently for later reference. There are, however, several other benefits of taking the time and effort to write up a research study.

First, as many writing texts note, writing is a way of thinking. Taking care to find the right words, to make clear and direct links between findings and the evidence they are drawn from, and to articulate what should happen next all require careful and precise thinking. The writing process helps researchers note gaps and inconsistencies in their

thinking and to crystallize what they have experienced and learned. As someone[1] once said, "How do I know what I think until I see what I said?" Writing is worthwhile, then, even when the researcher is the only one who will see the summary because it functions to help the writer clarify her thoughts.

Once something is written, however, the fact is that it becomes easy to share, and sharing produces another range of benefits. Drafts are useful in peer debriefing and member checking. When words are fixed on a page, it is easier for others to see just what the researcher intends to say and to think through their own reactions. Sentences and phrases can be revisited and adjustment, or objections or confirmations, offered. Written drafts are the easiest and most reliable way to share thinking, and they provide an easy way for others to reflect and comment on the researcher's thinking. Comments on drafts from a variety of audiences can help ensure that the final product is clear and credible.

Benefits to wider communities

While some research projects may originally be intended only for the researcher's own purposes, as when a teacher researches a classroom issue, others may nevertheless benefit from reading about them. It's always useful to see how someone else has addressed a problem we are struggling with. Knowing how others have defined and addressed a problem or situation they are experiencing can provide readers with greater insights into their own circumstances and new ideas for possible interventions. Indeed, one of the greatest potential benefits of action research is that it allows practitioners who would not normally have the opportunity to interact and learn from each other to share their questions and experiences, advancing the knowledge base and expertise of the larger professional community. Thus, potential audiences for action research reports include those in the immediate community—peers, other stakeholders, local authorities—as well as those who may be far distant—in other regions, states or nations.

Typical Characteristics of a Written Report

Components

While many people are uncomfortable with formal writing, most feel comfortable telling stories. The task of writing up an action research study is less formidable than it may sound, because such reports most often resemble story telling much more than the formal and often jargon-laden reports of positivist research. Most often, reports of action research have a conversational tone and simply do a good job of telling the story of the research. Although the finished products are as individualized as their authors, articles generally contain the same components. These include:

Background of the study. What made the researcher undertake this study? Why is its subject important? How did these things grow out of the researcher's personal values, experience, or context? Background information helps the reader know something about the researcher's perspective and goals.

Literature review, if one has been completed. What have other studies had to say on this question? How did they inform study design or interpretation of the data? How are the findings of this study similar to or different from those of other studies?

Overview of the research methods. What were the sources of data? How and why were they selected? Who were the participants? How were they selected? What process did the researcher use to analyze the data? What efforts did the researcher make to enhance the credibility of the findings (member checking, for example)?

Findings. What assertions can the researcher make based on the evidence collected? What kinds of evidence support each finding? What commonalities and what exceptions did the researcher identify relevant to findings?

Theorizing. How does the researcher interpret the findings? What does the researcher think the findings mean?

Action plan. What happens next? Who will do it? On what schedule?

Final reflections. The researcher's last word on overall significance of the project or other points she would like to make.

Components can appear in any order (though they often follow the order above), and they can take a wide variety of forms. In general, however, each component serves a particular purpose useful in helping readers develop a good understanding of events the researcher is reporting. The

following paragraphs explain the purpose of each component, with illustrations taken from an action research report written by Stella Marinakos, a science teacher in northeastern Pennsylvania.

The purpose of providing *background information* is to help readers better understand the work and enable them to make judgments about it. For example, explaining the impetus for a study often helps readers see the link between real-world experience and the research topic. Stella, for example, opened her report with a sampling of disquieting remarks she frequently heard from colleagues (Figure 5).

FIGURE 5: BACKGROUND INFORMATION EXCERPTS

Comments from colleagues that caught Stella's attention:
"He behaves in science class because he likes science."
"He asks questions in your class because science is a 'boys' class.'"
"She asks questions in your class? She likes science?"
"He speaks to you? He never speaks to me. That's because you teach science."

Her own background:
I have been teaching in a relatively rural town in Pennsylvania for 17 years, 13 of which have been in an eighth grade science classroom.

Importance of the study:
So often, I have heard my colleagues make comments about the gendered image of science. This is understandable considering how social stereotypes impact the field of science, as well as engineering, mathematics, and technology. From the lack of female representation in the content of science books and the assumptions that math and science are subjects that boys like to the under-representation of women in science, engineering, and technology professions, there have been issues associated with this gendered image.

Because other teachers may have similarly heard stereotypical remarks about their disciplines voiced by colleagues, the quotes are likely to signal immediately to many readers that she will describe a situation similar to one they have experienced.

Similarly, a description of the context of the study—urban junior high or kindergarten classroom, in an affluent community or a poor community—allows the reader to make judgments about how closely the context might resemble their own, or about how a particular context might have influenced the researcher's perspective. It's especially important in interpretivist work for researchers to be clear about the values and commitments they bring to a study so that readers can consider whether others with

different values and perspectives might have read the data differently.

Incorporating information from *literature reviews* helps readers see connections between a particular study and related work that has come before, enlarging their understanding of the issue overall. Literature review summaries are most often incorporated into written reports at the point they occurred during the research. That is, if a researcher did a literature review before beginning data collection, she might include a summary near the beginning of the article. If the review were completed later in the research process, a summary might be incorporated after the findings to explain links between the study being reported and earlier work. Or, as Stella did, a researcher might summarize findings from other studies early in the paper and refer to them again in discussing her own results (Figure 6).

FIGURE 6: LITERATURE REVIEW EXCERPTS

What did other studies have to say on this question?

Studies show that there are gaps between boys and girls in terms of performance and achievement, as well as interest in science (Alexakos and Antoine, 2003). However, even with all the documentation about these inequities, the gendered image prevails. Even within the realm of science, there is gender-based stereotyping. Farenga (1998) suggests that "both boys and girls perceive physical science and technology-related subjects as appropriate for boys to study" (p. 55). The same study suggested that life sciences were "appropriate subjects for girls to study" (p. 55).

How are the findings of this study similar to or different from those of other studies?

I was curious see how my results compared to a gender and science study conducted by Breakwell, Vignoles, and Robertson (2003). In their study, they found that girls who liked science scored themselves higher on masculine traits while boys who liked science rated themselves higher on feminine traits. My results did not coincide with their results. With the exception of one category, in my research, girls rated themselves higher than boys in feminine, masculine, and gender non-specific traits.

The discussion of *methods* helps readers decide whether they think the study is trustworthy. To decide, they will want to know such things as how much data was collected, from whom, and what specific links the researcher made between data and findings. For example, the statement "We found that discrimination based on sexual orientation is not an issue in our community, because it was never mentioned as a concern in any data" clearly explains the

researchers' thinking in moving from data to interpretation, allowing readers to decide whether or not they agree with it. Detailing methods also offers readers ideas for how they might implement similar studies in their own communities. Some of Stella's detailed presentation of her methods are presented in Figure 7.

FIGURE 7: RESEARCH METHODOLOGY EXCERPTS

What were the sources of data?

The survey was completed anonymously by 113 students. I read the survey to all students to help those who had difficulty. The students provided their sex and age and were asked to answer the following questions:

1. Overall, how much do you like science? Explain your answer.
2. Should every student take science? Explain your answer.
3. How would you describe a student who likes science? List as many characteristics as you can.
4. How would you describe a student who does not like science? List as many characteristics as you can.

Then, students rated themselves on 34 gender-specific and gender nonspecific traits. The five-point scales used by the students to rate how much they like or do not like science and how they rated themselves on the traits can be found in Appendix A.

What process did the researcher use to analyze the data?

When the surveys were completed I organized the surveys by gender and the five-point rating scale, i.e., 0, 1, 2, 3, and 4. At that point, I was ready to begin analyzing my data. That's when the fun began because I felt it was necessary to calculate every possible aspect of the study. These included:

- the average age of all students,
- the average age for the girl subgroup,
- the average for the boy subgroup,
- the average rating of liking or not liking science by gender,
- the average rating for each of the 34 character traits by gender *and* by rating for liking or not liking science (0, 1, 2, 3, and 4), and
- a frequency distribution for the reasons why students liked or disliked science by gender *and* by rating for liking science or not liking science (0, 1, 2, 3, and 4).

And obviously, readers also want to know the findings of the study. What new information did the researcher uncover? What does the researcher theorize that those findings mean? And, perhaps most important of all: What's next? What's the *action plan*? While it's important to detail everything leading up the findings so that the reader can assess trustworthiness and relevance of the work, the heart

of a research reports comes in answer to the questions "So what did you learn, what do you make of it, and what will you do now?" Partial sample answers from Stella's study appear in Figure 8.

FIGURE 8: FINDINGS, THEORIZING, AND ACTION PLAN EXCERPTS

What assertions can the researcher make based on the evidence collected?
What commonalities did the researcher identify?

Participants were asked to describe students who like science and those who do not like science. The lists of characteristics for both were rather lengthy and there was a great deal of overlap between the characteristics stated by boys and girls. The characteristics are summarized in Table 7. When I reviewed the surveys, it was interesting to see how often the stereotypical comments like "geek, nerd, and weird" were used in describing students who liked science.

What might findings mean?

With the exception of one category, in my research, girls rated themselves higher than boys in feminine, masculine, and gender non-specific traits. I am not sure exactly what this means as I am not a psychologist or sociologist; however, I would think that the girls feel strongly about who they are. I wonder, does this translate into being confident?

What are the next steps?

- The knowledge I gained about my students will help me improve my instruction. However, what is more important is to identify and eliminate gendered comments and situations that persist in our schools. The purveyors of such behaviors oftentimes are unaware of their actions. Hopefully, my research and the discussions that follow when I share it will educate the educators who unknowingly promote gendered actions.
- I will revise and repeat a self-reflection inventory in which students assess themselves in terms of reading and mathematics issues as they relate to learning science. Another activity will evaluate students in terms of Gardner's multiple intelligences.

Finally, the writer has the option of adding any *reflection* that can offer the reader still more food for thought. For example, action researchers are often refreshingly candid about how the work changed their earlier, unreflective assumptions and attitudes or how excited they are at the possibilities the study has opened. They might comment as well on lessons they learned about the value of action research, its impact on participants, or any other element of their experience. Virtually anything researchers consider worthwhile can be included in action research articles.

Stella's final comments are typical of those many teacher action researchers make when they conclude their first study:

> The most important lesson for me was to recognize and accept that teacher research does not have to be difficult, overly-detailed, or overly structured to be meaningful.... My experience indicates that if a systematic approach has been laid out, any investigation will be conducted efficiently and thoroughly; and, most importantly, the teacher will learn something that will help improve his or her teaching.

The fact that there is no single right answer in an action research study and that practitioners always seek first information for their own purposes means any ending reflection is an appropriate one.

One final component is possible, depending upon the study. If the researcher created special data collection tools—interview questions, or surveys, for example—copies should be included in appendices at the end of the report. As noted earlier, how a question is worded can shape responses, and readers often want to see the specific questions asked to judge their appropriateness for themselves.

Voice and format

Reports of action research studies vary widely in format and tone; there is no single genre for such work despite the fact that the same types of information generally appear. Most often, as noted above, the reports sound very like narrative essays where researchers report their experiences using a personal and informal tone, often speaking in metaphorical terms of their research *adventure* or *journey*. Stella's final report, for example, included very funny parenthetical remarks reflecting the difficulties she was having as a scientist moving from a positivist to an interpretivist paradigm—which cleverly demonstrated her additional finding that a first attempt at action research may be difficult for anyone trained in positivist research. For example, she found numerical data so appealing and reassuring that she had a constant battle not to include every single statistic she could produce just because she could produce it:

> The average age for the 113 students who took the survey was 13.65 years, which is typical for students in eighth

grade. Girls had a higher average for liking science than boys with a mean rating of 2.33. I just can't stay away from the decimals. One of my colleagues wanted to know how old a student was before he or she was 13.65 years. Too funny! I really need to be careful when I get out of here because my eyes will need to adjust...I'm still in the positivist closet.

The more readable an action research report is, the more likely it is to engage and influence others, so creativity can be a valuable element in a written report.

However, if the purpose of a study requires that it be persuasive to a more traditional, authoritative audience, it can also be shaped to more closely resemble a traditional research report. There is no reason interpretivist work can't be described under traditional segment headings like "Background of the Study" or "Research Methodology" in a typical report format. As in all writing, audience and purpose will help the writer choose among options.

There is, however, a good reason that a formal report format is not the norm in action research. The action researcher is always an insider who brings to the study an intimate understanding of the research context. Action research stands in direct opposition to traditional positivist research, which casts the researcher as a neutral observer who distances himself from events to maintain some hypothetical objectivity. In direct contrast, insider researchers are expected to describe exactly the kind of detail that positivist researchers take care to exclude. More specifically, they are expected to use their familiarity with the context to help the reader understand the unique elements of the situation—to help the reader grasp how certain events actually felt to the people involved, for example. An example from Stringer (2004) provides a nasty, but apt, illustration of the difference:

> Writing evocative accounts entails more than the bland reporting of events. It requires report writers to find the textual means to evoke those forms of understanding. A government report that referred to the "inadequate sewage" in a school failed to evoke an understanding of the stench of excreta and the parents' ongoing fear for their children's health. (129)

Rather than avoiding emotion, reports of action research seek to invite readers into the events by vividly portraying them—by calling attention to the stench of uncontained sewage and to parents' dismay and fears when authorities

place their children's health in danger by failing to correct such an egregious problem. For the interpretivist researcher, leaving out such detail constitutes not objectivity but a misrepresentation of the experience that they are uniquely qualified to report. As Stringer notes, "Objective reports are sometimes dangerously uninformative" (Stringer, 2004, 129). For many writers, the challenge of finding the words to evoke the lived experience is an engaging and creative experience that provides great satisfaction—and often freedom. Because so much of the writing they may have been forced to complete has been bland, dry and sterile, many action researchers find unexpected joy in the telling of their stories.

The best way to imagine the many possibilities for written reports of action research is to read a wide selection of them—an easy task, since they are abundant and easy to access. The Resources section contains links to on-line collections as well as citations for print collections. Browsing among the many studies that have already been published will no doubt introduce readers to kindred spirits whose work will offer useful models for tone and format.

Alternatives to Writing

While, as noted above, researchers should always record projects in writing at least for their own later reference, writing is not the only way to share a study with a wider audience. Several other possibilities include the following.

Electronic presentations

Such presentation programs as Microsoft's PowerPoint have made it easy to compose slide presentations that can include not only text but also photos, charts and other illustrations. Key points of the report can be summarized and outlined in the presentation, while the researcher verbally tells the story of the research more dynamically. Such presentations are useful in sharing the work face-to-face with interested groups.

Poster presentations

The poster presentation is common to academic conferences, but it can be used in other venues as well. A primary example would be a school district that supported teacher research system-wide and held an annual day for teachers to share their work in poster sessions. Posters typically have a very few sentences summarizing the key points of a study, sometime with illustrations or photographs to provide illustration or to draw attention. Many posters are displayed in a room, with creators standing by them as visitors wander the aisles, stopping to chat with presenters whose work they find of interest. Poster sessions provide a valuable opportunity for researchers and interested others to have one-on-one or small group in-person conversations. The Resources section includes a link to advice on creating good posters.

Performances

Interpretivist research has sparked a great deal more creativity than the positivist approach stressing neutrality and objectivity can allow. Since interpretive research is...well...interpretive, it has been a short journey from creative written texts to other kinds of creative/interpretive products. Some researchers have captured their work in such forms as drama, dance or song. For example, a researcher whose project revealed a great deal about student bullying in a school might write a script for a student play informed by the results of the research. When the play is presented to the school audience, the findings are in essence shared with the community at large, with insights into the effects on various persons being made evident through the characters in the play. Or, students who engaged with a teacher in a research project about values of the school community might paint a mural depicting the values their research identified.

With the versatility and availability of electronic resources, similar products can be captured and shared in electronic format in collages, videos, and other creative products.

Formats for sharing will be determined by the researcher's objectives and audiences as well as his own skills, interests and abilities. Limitations may come from within those parameters but are not imposed by norms of the action research community. A nice collection of action research reports in a variety of presentation formats—including several extremely creative ones—appears in Chapter 8 of Stringer's *Action Research in Education* (2004).

Opportunities for Sharing

Local audiences are as close as the breakfast table, the lunch room, or the study hall. Anyone can be asked "Do

you have a couple minutes to read something I've written and talk it over with me?" Interesting conversations can confirm the value of a researcher's work and provide energy to continue with the next study. Of course, the "anyone" can just as easily be a person or group with some influence: a supervisor, an administrator, a group of colleagues or parents or students. As the researcher's confidence grows, reaching a wider audience may become an objective.

Most often reaching these wider audiences generally includes "publishing" a written piece—perhaps in traditional print outlets but increasingly in electronic formats. Many of these are catalogued in the Resources section; the following list is simply an overview to indicate various types of possibilities.

Organizational meetings and publications

All kinds of organizations have routine meetings. Schools have in-service days, for example, and community groups, like Lions clubs or a Chamber of Commerce, meet regularly as well. Depending upon a researcher's topic, one or more groups might be interested in hearing about a study and its results. A study that indicated lack of affordable child care was affecting student school attendance, for example, might be of interest to several audiences, including community officials and church groups in addition to school personnel. A quick check with the person responsible for scheduling presentations at meetings can readily indicate whether or not there may be interest in and opportunity for sharing a study. Often, schedulers are happy to have volunteers.

Similarly, many organizations have newsletters and other documents that report on organizational activities and related topics of interest. Editors of such publications often have difficulty soliciting information and articles; many would be delighted to receive a relevant research report. Such sharing opportunities can be particularly important to a researcher who wants to promote an idea that would require the participation and support of multiple stakeholders—as would an effort to increase the amount of affordable day care available in a community.

Action research journals

There are print and online journals devoted to publishing action research reports. These journals, like all

journals, generally make guidelines for authors available from their websites and inside each issue. Such guidelines make clear the purpose of the journal and detail practicalities like word count and document format. An author planning to submit an article to *any* journal, print or electronic, is well advised to browse previous issues for a sense of the types of articles a particular journal may accept and to read the authors' guidelines carefully.

Local, state and national conferences and journals

Many national organizations—the International Reading Association (IRA), for example, and the Association for Supervision and Curriculum Development (ASCD)—are umbrella organizations that include many state and regional affiliates. Both national groups and their affiliates routinely hold conferences, often inviting persons interested in doing conference presentations to submit proposals. Depending upon the particular conference, papers, posters and creative projects may all be welcome. Many conferences, in fact, stress the option of creative presentations because their members are interested in breaking out of the typical "talking head" format. A check of organizational websites (listed in the Resources section) will provide information on upcoming conference themes, presentation formats, proposal requirements, and deadlines.

Similarly, national organizations and their affiliates generally publish their own **peer-reviewed journals**. So, for example, ASCD publishes *Educational Leadership,* and its Pennsylvania affiliate publishes *Pennsylvania Educational Leadership*. State and regional journals generally have a higher acceptance rate than national publications and are a good place for the novice researcher to begin submitting early efforts. An author unsure of whether a particular journal would welcome an action research report should consult its guidelines for authors, browse through earlier issues, and/or email the editor with questions.

Peer-Reviewed Journals

Journals that base the decision to publish or not on reviews of manuscripts completed by outside experts. Many reviewers offer writers good suggestions revising and improving an article.

A word on rejection

While publishing action research articles is a goal within reach of many practitioners, they may avoid submitting their work for fear it will be rejected. While rejection is a possibility, it is not one that should deter a researcher from the goal of publication. There are more writers than there are outlets for publication, so rejection is to be expected. Although no one feels good about it, often the most appro-

priate response is not to despair but to put the article in a new envelope and send it to another publication, trying again. Sometimes the piece will benefit from revision, and a professional critique from a journal's reviewers can help the author/s improve it. And sometimes, the writing is fine and the reviewer is the problem:

> We've received much helpful advice from caring editorial board members and reviewers from publishers. But we've also received pages of snotty insults from reviewers... A vicious or just plain lousy response to your work isn't a reflection on your writing—it's a reflection on the pettiness and unprofessionalism of the reviewer. (Hubbard & Power, 1999, p. 190).

The best way to avoid poor treatment is to focus on publications that specifically welcome action research articles, like those listed in the Resources section. Reading such publications is an excellent way to become familiar both with the genre of action research articles and with common features of articles published in a particular outlet. Another way to increase chances of success is to submit to smaller, more local publications at first.

No matter how or why, sharing is a habit that can help an action researcher and her work grow in multiple ways.

Some Thoughts on Community

Action researchers include professionals in a variety of roles—however, this closing word is primarily for teachers, who are among the most active practitioners engaging in such work.

Education writers and researchers often discuss the isolation that teachers experience during their workday, as they handle responsibilities for 20 to 200 students, with infrequent and crowded breaks in the action. Little time exists during the school day for teachers to engage in conversations about their daily classroom lives with colleagues, still less for extended conversations about practitioner research. The isolation that is part of every teacher's daily experience is reason enough to spend a few moments thinking about the issue of supportive communities for teacher researchers. Though teachers are the focus here, the general advice applies as well to other professions.

A researcher who works alone can soon develop doubt and lose faith: *Is any of this important? Is what I'm seeing actually here, or am I imagining things? This is never going to*

make sense; it's a jumbled mess and will never be more than a jumbled mess. Nothing I do will make any difference anyway. Such rough patches in the process are predictable and normal, but it's essential for researchers to have strategies and resources to push past them.

Many action researchers consider having a research community indispensable, even though (as noted earlier) many models don't consider or promote them as a necessary part of the work. Communities provide researchers with opportunities for discussions with like-minded others who share both an interest in inquiry and a passion to make things better. Research colleagues allow the individual researcher to discuss ideas, to ask for help, and to hear constructive criticism as well as genuine praise and encouragement. Such support can help a researcher persist over time and despite obstacles. Far less loftily, having a research group helps people meet self-imposed deadlines: no one wants to attend a research group meeting empty-handed, having done nothing new since the last meeting.

Although groups need a facilitator to arrange meeting times and places, a research community does not need a complicated infrastructure. It can be as modest as an informal group of a few colleagues who meet monthly over breakfast or dinner. Of course, it can also be much larger. Institutions may agree to sponsor research groups and provide time and other support for a regular meeting schedule and space. Still more ambitiously, a group might schedule annual retreats to reflect together on the work of the last year and to help each other sketch the shape of research for the year to come. In between regularly scheduled meetings, email allows for frequent, easy conversation anytime the researcher has a need. The only real requirements for a research community are that its members share an interest in using action research to make things better and that they come together dependably to support each other's efforts.

Context will shape possibilities, but a lone researcher who wants the support of a research community can choose to build one, taking one small step at a time. Every teacher has at least one ally in the building who always seems to be on the same side of any issue. Such an ally is a likely candidate for a first effort to enlist help. Even two researchers working together is an improvement over one working alone—and it's not likely to be long before they have ideas about who else might be interested, or before someone

else comes to ask to be included. Or, there are also many possibilities for finding colleagues outside an immediate context. Like-minded people are likely to turn up at professional gatherings, or in university courses, or even at social events like parties, concerts and community events. The researcher looking for colleagues simply needs to be willing to talk about his or her work and pay attention to who responds with interest.

The only prerequisite to forming a research group is the decision to make it happen.

Looking Forward

One great joy of action research is the freedom it offers practitioners. For example, the process offers a concrete strategy for finally *doing* something about the issue that has nagged the researcher for so long. Practitioners are free to choose any area of interest and to shape a question that best serves their own concerns; they are free to design the study as they think best; they are the ones who decide what in the data is important, what the data mean, and what should happen next. It is an empowering and inspiring process.

It is also a process that moves practitioners out of a subordinate position, where someone else decides what they should be doing, and into an authoritative position, where they assume responsibility for and control over their own actions and strategies. It is a process likely to benefit all stakeholders affected, but it is perhaps the researcher who is most immediately and intensely influenced by the professional freedoms experienced. Anyone can attempt an action research project and learn from it. And a very good time for anyone to begin would be—now.

GLOSSARY

Peer-Reviewed Journals: Journals that base the decision to publish or not on reviews of manuscripts completed by outside experts. Many reviewers offer writers good suggestions revising and improving an article.

NOTE

1. This quote has been variously ascribed to such diverse writers as Raymond Carver, E.M. Forster, and William James.

References and Further Resources

References

ActionResearch.net. Retrieved July 21, 2007, from http://people.bath.ac.uk/edsajw/

Adelman, C. (1993). Kurt Lewin and the origins of action research. *Educational Action Research, 1,* 7–24.

Anderson, G. L., Herr, K., & Nihlen, A. S. (1994). *Studying your own school: An educator's guide to qualitative practitioner research.* Thousand Oaks, Calif.: Corwin Press.

Atwell, N. (1987). *In the middle: Writing, reading, and learning with adolescents.* Upper Montclair, NJ: Boynton/Cook.

Carr, W. (1980). The gap between theory and practice. *Journal of Further and Higher Education, 4*(1), 60–69.

Carr, W., & Kemmis, S. (1986). *Becoming critical: Education, knowledge and action research.* Philadelphia, PA: Falmer Press.

Centre for Action Research in Professional Practice (CARPP). Retrieved July 21, 2007, from http://www.bath.ac.uk/carpp/

ChildStats.gov. (n.d.). Child poverty and family income. Retrieved August 2, 2007, from http://www.childstats.gov/americaschildren/ec01.asp

Clarke, A. & Erickson, G. (Eds.). (2003). *Teacher inquiry: Living the research in everyday practice.* London: RoutledgeFalmer.

Cochran-Smith, M., & Lytle, S. L. (1990). Research on teaching and teacher research: The issues that divide. *Educational Researcher, 19*(2), 2–10.

Cochran-Smith, M., & Lytle, S. L. (1993). *Inside/outside: Teacher research and knowledge*. New York: Teachers College Press.

Cochran-Smith, M., & Lytle, S. L. (1999). The teacher research movement: A decade later [Electronic Version]. *Educational Researcher, 28*, 15–25. Retrieved August 3, 2007 from JSTOR.

Collier, J. (1945). United States Indian administration as a laboratory of ethnic relations. *Social Research,* 265–303.

Corey, S. M., & Horace Mann-Lincoln Institute of School Experimentation. (1953). *Action research to improve school practices.* New York: Bureau of Publications, Teachers College, Columbia University.

Creswell, J. (2002). *Educational research: Planning, conducting, and evaluating quantitative and qualitative research.* Saddle River, NJ: Pearson Education.

Dana, N. F., & Yendol-Silva, D. (2003). *The reflective educator's guide to classroom research.* Thousand Oaks, CA: Corwin Press.

Denzin, N. K., & Lincoln, Y. S. (2000). The discipline and practice of qualitative research. In N. K. Denzin & Y. S. Lincoln (Eds.), *Handbook of qualitative research.* Thousand Oaks, CA: Sage.

Dewey, J. (1916). Democracy and education: An introduction to the philosophy of education [Electronic Version], xii, 434 p. Retrieved June 6, 2007 from http://www.worldwideschool.org/library/books/socl/education/democracyandeducation/toc.html

Dewey, J. (1933). *How we think : A restatement of the relation of reflective thinking to the educative process.* New York: D. C. Heath/.

Freire, P. (1970). *Pedagogy of the oppressed.* New York: Seabury Press.

Freire, P. (1997). *Mentoring the mentor: A critical dialogue with Paulo Freire.* New York: Peter Lang.

Heath, S. B. (1983). *Ways with words: Language, life, and work in communities and classrooms.* Cambridge [Cambridgeshire] ; New York: Cambridge University Press.

Hendricks, C. (2006). *Improving schools through action research: A comprehensive guide for educators.* Boston: Pearson/Allyn and Bacon.

Herbert, A., Stephen, K., Robin, M., & Ortrun, Z.-S. (2002). The concept of action research. *The Learning Organization, 9*(3/4), 125–132.

Holly, M. L., Arhar, J. M., & Kasten, W. C. (2005). *Action research for teachers: Traveling the yellow brick road* (2nd ed.). Upper Saddle River, N.J.: Pearson/Merrill/Prentice Hall.

Hubbard, R. & Power, B. M. (1999). *Living the questions: A guide for teacher-researchers.* York, ME: Stenhouse.

Kemmis, S. (1993). Action research and social movement: A challenge for policy research. *Education Policy Analysis Archives, 1*(1).

Kincheloe, J. L. (1991). *Teachers as researchers: Qualitative inquiry as a path to empowerment.* London: Falmer Press.

Kuhn, T. S. (1962). *The structure of scientific revolutions.* Chicago: University of Chicago Press.

Lewin, K. (1946). Action research and minority problems. *The Journal of Social Issues, 2*(4), 34–46.

Lincoln, Y. S., & Guba, E. G. (1985). *Naturalistic inquiry.* Beverly Hills, Calif.: Sage Publications.

McTaggart, R. (1991). *Action research: A short modern history.* Victoria: Deakin University.

McTaggart, R. (1994). Participatory action research: Issues in theory and practice. *Educational Action Research, 2*(3), 313–337.

Miller, S. K. (2001). Lessons from Tony: Betrayal and trust in teacher research [Electronic Version]. *The Quarterly, 23.* Retrieved August 15, 2007 from http://www.nwp.org/cs/public/print/resource/149

Mohr, M. M., Rogers, C., Sanford, B., Nocerino, M. A., MacLean, M. S., & Clawson, S. (2004). *Teacher research for better schools.* New York: Teachers College Press.

Noffke, S. (1997). Professional, personal and political dimensions of action research. In *Review of Research in Education* (Vol. 22, pp. 305–343). Washington, DC: AERA.

Noffke, S. E., & Stevenson, R. B. (Eds.). (1995). *Educational action research: Becoming practically critical.* New York: Teachers College Press.

Sanford, N. (1970). Whatever happened to action research? *The Journal of Social Issues, 26*(4), 3–23.

Schmuck, R. A. (2006). *Practical action research for change* (2nd ed.). Thousand Oaks, CA: Corwin Press.

Schön, D. A. (1983). *The reflective practitioner: How professionals think in action.* New York: Basic Books.

Sherman, R. R., & Webb, R. B. (1997). *Qualitative research in education: Focus and methods.* Philadelphia: Falmer.

Shumsky, A. (1958). *The action research way of learning: An approach to in-service education.* New York: Teachers College.

Stenhouse, L. (1975). *An introduction to curriculum research and development.* London: Heinemann.

Stenhouse, L. (1981). What counts as research? [Electronic Version]. *British Journal of Educational Studies,* 29, 103–114. Retrieved June 13, 2007 from Ebsco Host, June 13, 2007.

Stenhouse, L., Rudduck, J., & Hopkins, D. (1985). *Research as a basis for teaching: Readings from the work of Lawrence Stenhouse.* Portsmouth, NH: Heinemann.

Stringer, E. T. (2004). *Action research in education.* Upper Saddle River, NJ: Pearson/Merrill/Prentice Hall.

Taba, H., & Noel, E. (1957). *Action research: A case study.* Washington, DC: Association for Curriculum & Supervision.

Tomal, D. R. (2003). *Action research for educators.* Lanham, MD.: ScarecrowEducation.

Whitehead, J. (1989). Creating a living educational theory from questions of the kind, 'How do I improve my practice?" [Electronic Version]. *Cambridge Journal of Education,* 19, 41–52. Retrieved July 21, 2007 from http://people.bath.ac.uk/edsajw/writings/livtheory.html

Whitehead, J. (1989). How do we improve research-based professionalism in education?: A question which includes action research, educational theory and the politics of educational knowledge. *Britiish Educational Research Journal, 15*(1), 3–17.

Zeichner, K., & Noffke, S. (2001). Practitioner research. In V. Richardson (Ed.), *The handbook of research on teaching* (pp. 298–330). Washington, DC: American Educational Research Association.

Zeni, J. (1998). A guide to ethical issues and action research. *Educational Action Research, 6*(1), 9–19. Available http://www.informaworld.com/smpp/content?content=10.1080/09650799800200053

Zeni, J. (2001). *Ethical issues in practitioner research.* New York: Teachers College Press.

Action Research Websites

Action Research Electronic Reader (Ian Huges and Bob Dick, Southern Cross University, Australia)
http://www.scu.edu.au/schools/gcm/ar/arr/arow/default.html

ActionResearch.net (Jack Whitehead, Bath University, UK)
http://people.bath.ac.uk/edsajw

Action and Research Open Web (University of Sydney, Australia)
http://www2.fhs.usyd.edu.au/arow/

The Action Research Laboratory at Highland Park High School (Illinois)
http://www.dist113.0rg/hphs/action/table_of_contents.htm

Action Research Network Ireland
http://www.iol.ie/~rayo/AR_Web/index.html

Action Research Resources (Bob Dick, Southern Cross University, Australia)
http://www.scu.edu.au/schools/gcm/ar/arhome.html

American Educational Research Association (AERA) Action Research Special Interest Group
http://coe.westga.edu/arsig/

Center for Action Research in Professional Practice (CARPP)
http://www.bath.ac.uk/carpp

Center for Collaborative Action Research (CCAR) (Pepperdine University)
http://cadres.pepperdine.edu/ccar/

Center for School Improvement (University of Florida)
http://education.ufl.edu/web/index.php?pid=903

Collaborative Action Research Network (CARN) (Manchester Metropolitan University, UK)
http://www.did.stu.mmu.ac.uk/carn/

COMM-ORG
http://comm-org.wisc.edu/research.htm

Community Research Partnerships (University of Toronto)
http://www.urbancentre.utoronto.ca/curp/participatory.html

Data Center: Impact Research for Social Justice
http://www.datacenter.org/index.htm

East St. Louis Action Research Project (University of Illinois at Urbana-Champaign and St. Louis Community Groups)
http://www.eslarp.uiuc.edu/

The Free Child Project
http://www.freechild.org/PAR.htm

Madison Metropolitan School District Classroom Action Research (WI)
http://www.madison.k12.wi.us/sod/car/carhomepage.html

Education as Inquiry: A Teacher Action Research Project (Judith M. Newman)
http://www.lupinworks.com/ar/index.html

The Institute for Community Research
http://www.incommunityresearch.org/research/yari.htm

Jean McNiff's Homepage
http://www.jeanmcniff.com/

Living the Question
http://www.livingthequestion.com/

National Writing Project, Resource Topics: Teacher research/inquiry
http://www.nwp.org/cs/public/print/resource_topic/teacher_research_inquiry

Research for Action (Philadelphia)
http://www.researchforaction.org/index.html

Teacher Research (George Mason University)
http://gse.gmu.edu/research/tr/

Teacher Research—Action Research Resources (University of California Educational Research Center)
http://ucerc.edu/teacherresearch/teacherresearch.html

Web Links to Participatory Action Research Sites (Goshen College)
http://www.goshen.edu/soan/soan96p.html

Youth Action Research Group (Georgetown University)
http://socialjustice.georgetown.edu/research/yarg/

Useful Online Research Tools

Action Research Network
http://actionresearch.altec.org/
A site where teacher action researchers can share their work and read the work of others.

Community Tool Box
http://ctb.ku.edu/WST/initiatives_show.jsp?initiative_id=97
Information and tools useful in building and maintaining Community Action-Research Centers

Focus Groups—How to Run Them (Webcredible)
http://www.webcredible.co.uk/user-friendly-resources/web-usability/focus-groups.shtml
Basic and direct advice on successfully managing a focus group; active researchers are not the target audience, but all advice applies.

Free Assessment Summary Tool (FAST)
http://www.getfast.ca/
A free online system that allows teachers to design and administer a questionnaire to collect anonymous feedback from their students.

Responses are automatically summarized and consolidated and can be downloaded into a Microsoft Excel spreadsheet.

Providing Poster Sessions (UNDMJ Center for Teaching Excellence)
http://cte.umdnj.edu/career_development/career_posters.cfm
This page, sponsored by a New Jersey university for dental and medical education, lists 19 useful links to advice on creating research posters. Though the advice generally uses examples from quantitative research, it applies equally to qualitative research.

Survey and Questionnaire (StatPac Inc.)
http://www.statpac.com/surveys/
An online tutorial in plain language with helpful advice on designing surveys and questionnaires.

Survey Monkey.com
http://www.surveymonkey.com/
A site that allows researchers to design and administer surveys online. Free surveys are limited to 10 questions and 100 respondents. More extensive services, including the ability to print copies of the survey and results, are available for a modest monthly fee.

Weft QDA (Qualitative Data Analysis)
http://www.pressure.to/qda/
A tool to assist in the analysis of such textual data as interview transcripts and field notes.

Edited Volumes of Action Research Articles

Anderson, F. & Moore, M. (Eds.) (2004). *Action research for inclusive education: Changing places, changing practices, changing minds.* New York: RoutledgeFalmer.

Atweh, B., Kemmis, S., & Weeks, P. (Eds.) (1998). *Action research in practice: Partnerships for social justice in education.* London: Routledge.

Burnaford, G. E., Fischer, J., & Hobson, D. (Eds.). (2001) *Teachers doing research: The power of action through inquiry (*2nd ed.*).* Mahwah, NJ: Lawrence Erlbaum Associates.

Clarke, A. & Erickson, G. (Eds.). (2003). *Teacher inquiry: Living the research in everyday practice.* London: RoutledgeFalmer.

Connelly, F., and Clandinin, D. (Eds.). (1999). *Shaping a professional identity: Stories of educational practice.* New York: Teachers College Press.

Dadds, M. & Hart, S. (Eds.) (2001). *Doing practitioner research differently.* London: RoutledgeFalmer.

Hollingsworth, S. (Ed.) (1997). *International action research: A casebook for educational reform.* London: Falmer Press.

Meyers, E. & Rust, F. O. (Eds.) (2003). *Taking action with action research.* Portsmouth, NH: Heinemann.

Noffke, S. E. & Stevenson, R. (Eds.) (1995). *Educational action research: Becoming practically critical.* New York: Teachers College Press.

Foundational Works

Collier, J. (1945). United States Indian administration as a laboratory of ethnic relations. *Social Research*, 265–303.

Corey, S.M. (1953). *Action research to improve school practices*. New York: Teachers College Press.

Dewey, J. (1916). *Democracy and education: An introduction to the philosophy of education*. New York: Macmillan.

Dewey, J. (1933). *How we think: A restatement of the relation of reflective thinking to the educative process*. New York: D. C. Heath.

Freire, P. (1970). *Pedagogy of the oppressed*. New York: Seabury Press.

Lewin, K. (1946). Action research and minority problems. *The Journal of Social Issues, 2*(4), 34–46.

Schön, D. (1987). *Educating the reflective practitioner*. London: Jossey-Bass.

Shumsky, A. (1958). *The action research way of learning: An approach to in-service education*. New York: Teachers College.

Stenhouse, L. (1975). *An introduction to curriculum research and development*. London: Heinemann Education.

Taba, H. & Noel, E. (1957). *Action research: A case study*. Washington, DC: Association for Curriculum & Supervision.

Books and Articles on Action Research

Adelman, C. (1993). Kurt Lewin and the origins of action research. *Educational Action Research, 1*(1), 7–22.

Allen, L. & Calhoun, E. F. (1998). Schoolwide action research: Findings from six years of study. *Phi Delta Kappan 79*(9), 706.

Anderson, G. L. & Herr, K. (1999). The new paradigm wars: Is there room for rigorous practitioner knowledge in schools and universities? *Educational Researcher, 28*(5), 12–21+40.

Atwell, N. (1987). In the middle: Writing, reading, and learning with adolescents. Upper Montclair, NJ: Boynton/Cook.

Berge, B.M. & Ve, H. (2000). *Action research for gender equity*. Buckingham: Open University Press.

Brause, R. S., & Mayher, J. S. (1991). *Search and re-search: What the inquiring teacher needs to know*. London: Falmer Press.

Calhoun, E. (2002). Action research for school improvement. *Educational Leadership, 59*, 18–24.

Campbell, A. & Groundwater-Smith, S. (2007). *An ethical approach to practitioner research: Dealing with issues and dilemmas in action research*. London: Routledge.

Carr, W. & Kemmis, S. (1986). *Becoming critical: Education, knowledge, and action research*. London: Falmer Press.

Carson, T. (1990, Summer). What kind of knowing is critical action research? *Theory into Practice, 9*, 167–73.

Carson, T. & Sumara, D. (Eds.) (1997). *Action research as a living practice*. New York: Peter Lang.

Clift, R. Houston, W. R. & Pugach, M. (Eds.). (1990). *Encouraging reflective practice in education: An analysis of issues and programs*. New York: Teachers College Press.

Cochran-Smith, M. (1991). Learning to teach against the grain. *Harvard Educational Review, 67,* 279–310.

Cochran-Smith, M. & Lytle, S. L. (1990). Research on teaching and teacher research: The issues that divide. *Educational Researcher 19*(2), 2–10.

Cochran-Smith, M. & Lytle, S.L. (1993). *Inside/outside: Teacher research and knowledge*. New York: Teachers College Press.

Cochran-Smith, M. & Lytle, S.L. (1999). The teacher research movement: A decade later. *Educational Researcher, 28,* 15–25.

Dadds, M. (1995). *Passionate enquiry and school development: A story about teacher action research*. London: Falmer.

Dadds, M. (1996). Supporting practitioner research: A challenge. *Educational Action Research, 6*(1), 39–52.

Dana, N. F. (1995). Action research, school change, and the silencing of teacher voice. *Action in Teacher Education, 16*(4), 59–70.

Eisner, E. (1984). Can educational research inform educational practice? *Phi Delta Kappan, 65*(7), 447–452.

Elliott, J. & Adelman, C. (1973). Reflecting where the action is: The design of the Ford Teaching Project. *Education for Teaching, 92,* 8–20.

Elliott, J. (1987). Educational theory, practical philosophy, and action research. *British Journal of Educational Studies, 35*(2), 149–169.

Elliott, J. (1991). *Action research for educational change*. Philadelphia: Open University Press.

Foshay, A. W. (1994). Action research: An early history in the United States. *Journal of Curriculum and Supervision, 9,* 317–325.

Gitlin, A., & Thompson, A. (1995). Foregrounding politics in action research. *McGill Journal of Education, 30,* 131–147.

Gore, J. (1991). On silent regulation: Emancipatory action research in pre-service teacher education. *Curriculum Perspectives, 11*(4), 47–51.

Gore, J. & Zeichner, K. (1984). Action research and preservice teacher education: A case study from the U.S. *Teaching and Teacher Education, 7*(2), 119–136.

Haggarty, L. & Postlethwaite, K. (2003). Action research: A strategy for teacher change and school development? *Oxford Review of Education, 29*(4), 423–448.

Henson, K. T. (1996). Teachers as researchers. In J. Sikula (Ed.), *Handbook of research on teacher education* (2nd ed., 53–66). New York: Macmillan.

Hiebert, J., Gallimore, R., and Stigler, J. (2002). A knowledge base for the teaching profession. *Educational Researcher, 31,* 3–15.

Hollingsworth, S. (1994). *Teacher research and urban literacy education: Lessons and conversations in a feminist key*. New York: Teachers College Press.

Goswami, D. & Stillman, P. (Eds.) (1987). *Reclaiming the classroom: Teacher research as an agency for change*. Montclair, NJ: Boynton/Cook.

Hinchey, P., S., A., Demarco, N., & Fetchina, K. (1999). Sketching a self-portrait of skills instruction: Classroom research and accountability. *Language Arts, 77*(1), 19–26.

Johnson, S. & Proudford, C. (1994). Action research—who owns the process? *Educational Review, 46*(1), 3–14.

Kemmis, S. & McTaggart, R. (Eds.) (1988). *The action research reader* (3rd ed.). Geelong, Victoria, Australia: Deakin University Press.

Kincheloe, J.L. (1991) *Teachers as researchers: Qualitative inquiry as a path to empowerment.* London: Falmer Press.

Labaree, D. F. (1992). Power, knowledge, and the rationalization of teaching: A genealogy of the movement to professionalize teaching. *Harvard Educational Review, 62,* 123–154.

Lomax, P. & Parker, Z. (1995). Accounting for ourselves: The problematics of representing action research. *Cambridge Journal of Education, 25*(3), 301–14.

Lyons, N., & LaBoskey, V.K. (Eds.) (2002). *Narrative inquiry in practice.* New York: Teachers College Press.

McCutcheon, G., & Jung, B. (1990). Alternative perspectives on action research. *Theory into Practice, 29*(3), 144.

MacIntyre, C. (2000). *The art of action research in the classroom.* London: D. Fulton Publishers.

McNiff, Jean. (2002). *Action research: Principles and practice.* London: Routledge Falmer.

McTaggart, R. (1984). Action research and parent participation: Contradictions, concerns and consequences. *Curriculum Perspectives, 4*(2), 7–14.

McTaggart, R. (1991). *Action research: A short modern history.* Geelong, Victoria Australia: Deakin University Press.

McTaggart, R. (1994). Participatory action research: Issues in theory and practice. *Educational Action Research, 2,* 313–337.

McTaggart, R. (Ed.) (1997). *Participatory action research.* Albany, NY: SUNY Press.

Manning, B. H. & McLaughlin, H. J. (Eds.) (1995). Action research and teacher education [Special issue]. *Action in Teacher Education, 16*(4).

Miller, S. K. (2001). Lessons from Tony: Betrayal and trust in teacher research. Available from http://www.nwp.org/cs/public/print/resource/149

Mohr, M. M., Rogers, C. Sanford, B. Nocerino, M.A., MacLean, M. S. & Clawson, S. (2004). *Teacher research for better schools.* New York: Teachers College Press.

Nixon, J. (1987). The teacher as researcher: Contradictions and continuities. *Peabody Journal of Education, 64*(2), 20–32.

Noffke, S. (1997). Professional, personal and political dimensions of action research. In *Review of Educational Research 22,* 305–343.

Noffke, S. E. & Stevenson, R. B. (Eds.). (1995). *Educational action research: Becoming practically critical.* New York: Teachers College Press.

Peters, R. S. (1966). *Ethics and education.* Sydney, Australia: Allen & Unwin.

Rearick, M. L, & Feldman, A. (1999). Orientations, purposes, and reflection: A framework for understanding action research. *Teaching and Teacher Education, 15,* 333–349.

Saavedra, E. (1996). Teacher study groups: Context for transformative learning and action. *Theory into Practice, 35*(4), 271–277.

Schwalbach, E. M. (2003). *Value and validity in action research: A guidebook for reflective practitioners.* Lanham, MD: Scarecrow Press.

Steinberg, S. R. & Kincheloe, J. L. (1998). *Students as researchers: Creating classrooms that matter.* London: Falmer Press.

Stenhouse, L. (1981). What counts as research? *British Journal of Educational Studies, 29,* 102–122.

Stenhouse, L., Rudduck, J. & Hopkins, D. (1985). *Research as a basis for teaching: Readings from the work of Lawrence Stenhouse.* Portsmouth, NH: Heinemann.

Torrance, H. & Pryor, J. (2001). Developing formative assessment in the classroom: Using action research to explore and modify theory. *British Educational Research Journal, 27*(5), 615–631.

Torres, C. A. (1992). Participatory action research and popular education in Latin America. *Qualitative Studies in Education, 5,* 51–62.

Tripp, D. (1990). Socially critical action research. *Theory into Practice (29)*3, 158–166.

Walker, M. (1993). Developing the theory and practice of action research: A South African case. *Educational Action Research, 1*(1), 95–109.

Walker, M. (1995). Context, critique, and change: Doing action research in South Africa. *Educational Action Research, 3,* 9–27.

Weiner, G. (1989). Professional self-knowledge versus social justice: A critical analysis of the teacher-research movement. *British Educational Research Journal, 15*(1), 41–51.

Whitehead, J. (1989). How do we improve research-based professionalism in education? A question which includes action research, educational theory and the politics of educational knowledge. *British Educational Research Journal, 15*(1), 3–17.

Whitehead, J. (2000). How do I improve my practice? Creating and legitimating an epistemology of practice. *Reflective Practice, 1*(1), 91–104.

Whyte, W. F. (Ed.) (1990). *Participatory action research.* Thousand Oaks, CA: Sage.

Zeichner, K. (1991). Contradictions and tensions in the professionalization of teaching and the democratization of schools. *Teachers College Record, 92*(3), 363–379.

Zeichner, K. (1993). Connecting genuine teacher development to the struggle for social justice. *Journal of Education for Teaching, 17*(1), 5–20.

Zeichner, K. (1991). Contradictions and tensions in the professionalization of teaching and democratization of schools. *Teachers College Record, 92*(3), 363–379.

Zeichner, K. (1993). Action research: Personal renewal and social reconstruction. *Educational Action Research, 1*(2), 199–219.

Zeichner, K. (1995). Beyond the divide of teacher research and academic research. *Teachers and Teaching, Theory and Practice 1*(2), 153–172.

Zeichner, K. & Noffke, S. (2001). Practitioner research. In V. Richardson (Ed.), *The handbook of research on teaching* (pp. 298–330). Washington, DC: American Educational Research Association.

Action Research Textbooks

Anderson, G. L., Herr, K., & Nihlen, A. S. (1994). *Studying your own school: An educator's guide to qualitative practitioner research.* Thousand Oaks, CA: Corwin Press.

Dana, N. F. & Yendol-Silva, D. (2003). *The reflective educator's guide to classroom research: Learning to teach and teaching to learn through practitioner inquiry.* Thousand Oaks, CA: Corwin.

Hendricks, C. (2006). *Improving schools through action research: A comprehensive guide for educators.* New York: Pearson.

Holly, M. L., Arhar, J., & Kasten, W. (2005). *Action research for teachers: Traveling the yellow brick road.* Upper Saddle River, NJ: Pearson.

Hubbard, R. S. & Power, B. M. (1999). *Living the questions: A guide for teacher-researchers.* Portland, ME: Stenhouse.

Johnson, A. P. (2007). *A short guide to action research,* 3rd ed. Boston: Allyn and Bacon.

Koshy, V. (2005). *Action research for improving practice: A practical guide.* London: Paul Chapman Educational Publishing.

McNiff, J., Lomax, P. & Whitehead, J. (2003). *You and your action research project,* 2nd ed. New York: Routledge.

McNiff, J. & Whitehead, J. (2006). *All you need to know about action research.* Thousand Oaks, CA: Sage.

Mertier, C. A. (2005). *Action research: Teachers as researchers in the classroom.* Thousand Oaks, CA: Sage.

Phillips, D. K. & Carr, K. (2006). *Becoming a teacher through action research: Process, context, and self-study.* London: Routledge.

Sagor, R. (2000). *Guiding school improvement with action research.* Alexandria, VA: Association for Supervision and Curriculum Development.

Schmuck, R. A. (2006). *Practical action research for change (2nd ed.).* Thousand Oaks, CA: Corwin.

Stringer, E. T. (2007). *Action research in education,* (3rd ed.). Upper Saddle River, NJ: Prentice Hall.

Wallace, M. J. (1998). *Action research for language teachers.* Cambridge, England: Cambridge University Press.

Research Methodology and Documentation

American Educational Research Association. (2000). Ethical standards of the American Educational Research Association. Available http://www.aera.net/uploadedFiles/About_AERA/Ethical_Standards/EthicalStandards.pdf

Bullough, R. V. Jr, & Pinnegar, S. (2001). Guidelines for quality in autobiographical forms of self-study research. *Educational Research, 30*(3), 13–21.

Corbin, J. M., & Strauss, A. (2007). *Basics of qualitative research: Techniques and procedures for developing grounded theory* (3rd ed). Thousand Oaks, CA: Sage.

Creswell, J. W. (1997). *Qualitative inquiry and research design" Choosing among five traditions.* Thousand Oaks, CA: Sage.

Creswell, J. W. (2002). *Research design: Qualitative, quantitative, and mixed methods approached* (2nd ed.). Thousand Oaks, CA: Sage.

Denzin, N. K. & Lincoln, Y. S. (Eds.) (1998). *Collecting and interpreting qualitative materials.* Thousand Oaks, CA: Sage.

Denzin, N.K. & Lincoln, Y. S. (2000). The discipline and practice of qualitative research. In N. K. Denzin & Y.S. Lincoln (Eds.), *Handbook of qualitative research* (2nd ed., 1–28). Thousand Oaks, CA: Sage.

Denzin, N.K. & Lincoln, Y. S. (2003). *The landscape of qualitative research: Theories and issues* (2nd. Ed.). Thousand Oaks, CA: Sage.

Elliot, J. (1988). Education research and outsider-insider relations. *Qualitative Studies in Education, 1*(2), 155–166.

Ely, M. (1966). *Doing qualitative research: Circles within circles.* Philadelphia: Falmer.

Kemmis, S. & McTaggart, R. (2000). Participatory action research. In N. K. Denzin & Y.S. Lincoln (Eds.), *Handbook of qualitative research* (2nd ed., 567–605). Thousand Oaks, CA: Sage.

Krueger, R. A. & Casey, M. A. (2000). *Focus groups: A practical guide for applied research* (3rd ed.). Thousand Oaks, CA: Sage.

Lincoln, Y. S. & Guba, E. G. (1985). *Naturalistic inquiry.* Beverly Hills, CA: Sage.

Marshall, C. & Rossman, G. B. (2006). *Designing qualitative research (*4th ed.). Thousand Oaks, CA: Sage.

Merriam, S. B. (Ed.) (2002). *Qualitative research in practice: Examples for discussion and analysis.* San Francisco, CA: Jossey-Bass.

Miles, M. B. & Huberman, A. M. (1994). *Qualitative data analysis* (2nd ed.). Thousand Oaks, CA: Sage.

Perrin, R. (2007). *Pocket guide to APA Style* (2nd ed.). Boston: Houghton Mifflin.

Power, B. M. (1996). *Taking note: Improving your observational note taking.* York, ME: Stenhouse.

Reason, P. & Bradbury, H. (2001). *Handbook of action research.* Thousand Oaks, CA: Sage.

Schwandt, T. A. (2007). *The Sage dictionary of qualitative inquiry.* Thousand Oaks: Sage.

Zeichner, K. M. & Noffke, S. E. (2001). Practitioner research. In V. Richardson (Ed.), *Handbook of research on teaching* (4th Edition, 198–330). Washington, DC: American Educational Research Association.

Zeni, J. (1998). A guide to ethical issues and action research. *Educational Action Research, 6*(1), 9–19. Available http://www.informaworld.com/smpp/content?content=10.1080/09650799800200053

Zeni, J. (Ed.). (2001). *Ethical issues in practitioner research.* New York: Teachers College Press.

Education Organizations That Sponsor Conferences and Publications

American Association of School Administrators (AASA)
http://www.aasa.org

American Council on the Teaching of Foreign Languages (ACTFL)
http://www.actfl.org/i4a/pages/index.cfm?pageid=1

American Educational Research Association (AERA)
http://www.aera.net
(See especially relevant Special Interest Groups)

Association for Career and Technical Education (ACTE)
http://www.acteonline.org

Association for Supervision and Curriculum Development (ASCD)
http://www.ascd.org

Music Teachers National Association (MTNA)
http://www.mtna.org

National Art Education Association (NAEA)
http://www.naea-reston.org

National Association for the Education of Young Children (NAEYC)
http://www.naeyc.org

National Association for Music Education (MENC)
http://www.menc.org

National Council for Social Studies (NCSS)
http://www.socialstudies.org

International Conference on Teacher Research (ICTA)
http://www.nl.edu/academics/nce/ictr.cfm

International Reading Association (IRA)
http://www.reading.org

National Council of Teachers of English (NCTE)
http://www.ncte.org

National Council of Teachers of Math (NCTM)
http://www.nctm.org

National Middle School Association (NMSA)
http://www.nmsa.org

National Science Teacher Association (NSTA)
http://www.nsta.org

Peter Lang
PRIMERS
in Education

Peter Lang Primers are designed to provide a brief and concise introduction or supplement to specific topics in education. Although sophisticated in content, these primers are written in an accessible style, making them perfect for undergraduate and graduate classroom use. Each volume includes a glossary of key terms and a References and Resources section.

Other published and forthcoming volumes cover such topics as:

- Standards
- Popular Culture
- Critical Pedagogy
- Literacy
- Higher Education
- John Dewey
- Feminist Theory and Education

- Studying Urban Youth Culture
- Multiculturalism through Postformalism
- Creative Problem Solving
- Teaching the Holocaust
- Piaget and Education
- Deleuze and Education
- Foucault and Education

Look for more Peter Lang Primers to be published soon. To order other volumes, please contact our Customer Service Department:

    800-770-LANG (within the US)
    212-647-7706 (outside the US)
    212-647-7707 (fax)

To find out more about this and other Peter Lang book series, or to browse a full list of education titles, please visit our website:
    www.peterlang.com